How to use Explore

Issue 104

The 92 daily readings in this issue of *Explore* are designed to help you understand and apply the Bible as you read it each day.

It's serious!

We suggest that you allow 15 minutes each day to work through the Bible passage with the notes. It should be a meal, not a snack! Readings from other parts of the Bible can throw valuable light on the study passage. These cross-references can be skipped if you are already feeling full up, but will expand your grasp of the Bible. *Explore* uses the NIV2011 Bible translation, but you can also use it with the NIV1984 or ESV translations.

Sometimes a prayer section will encourage you to stop and pray through the lessons—but it is always important to allow time to pray for God's Spirit to bring his word to life, and to shape the way we think and live through it.

We're serious!

All of us who work on *Explore* share a passion for getting the Bible into people's lives. We fiercely hold to the Bible as God's word—to honour and follow, not to explain away.

1 Find a time you can read the Bible each day

2 Find a place where you can be quiet and think

3 Ask God to help you understand

4 Carefully read through the Bible passage for today

5 Study the verses with Explore, taking time to think

6 Pray about what you have read

thegoodbook COMPANY

BIBLICAL | RELEVANT | ACCESSIBLE

T0015724

Welcome to Explore

Tim Thornborough is the Publishing Director
at The Good Book Company

Being a Christian isn't a skill you learn, like carpentry or flower arranging. Nor is it a lifestyle choice, like the kind of clothes you wear, or the people you choose to hang out with. It's about having a real relationship with the living God through his Son, Jesus Christ. The Bible tells us that this relationship is like a marriage.

It's important to start with this, because many Christians view the practice of daily Bible reading as a Christian duty, or a hard discipline that is just one more thing to get done in our busy modern lives.

But the Bible is God speaking to us: opening his mind to us on how he thinks, what he wants for us and what his plans are for the world. And most importantly, it tells us what he has done for us in sending his Son, Jesus Christ, into the world. It's the way that the Spirit shows Jesus to us, and changes us as we behold his glory.

The Bible is not a manual. It's a love letter. And as with any love letter, we'll want to treasure it, and make time to read and re-read it, so we know we are loved, and discover how we can please the One who loves us. Here are a few suggestions for making your daily time with God more of a joy than a burden:

- *Time:* Find a time when you will not be disturbed, and when the cobwebs are cleared from your mind. Many people have found that the morning is the best time as it sets you up for the day. If you're not a "morning person", then last thing at night or a mid-morning break may suit you. Whatever works for you is right for you.

- *Place:* Jesus says that we are not to make a great show of our religion *(see Matthew 6:5-6)*, but rather, to pray with the door to our room shut. Some people plan to get to work a few minutes earlier and get their Bible out in an office or some other quiet corner.

- *Prayer:* Although *Explore* helps with specific prayer ideas from the passage, you should try to develop your own lists to pray through. Use the flap inside the back cover to help with this. And allow what you read in the Scriptures to shape what you pray for yourself, the world and others.

- *Share:* As the saying goes: *expression deepens impression.* So try to cultivate the habit of sharing with others what you have learned. Why not join our Facebook group to share your encouragements, questions and prayer requests? Search for *Explore: For your daily walk with God.*

And remember, *it's quality, not quantity, that counts:* better to think briefly about a single verse than to skim through pages without absorbing anything, because it's about developing your relationship with the living God. The sign that your daily time with God is real is when you start to love him more and serve him more wholeheartedly.

Finite

One of our chief problems in life is that we lack perspective. We get so engrossed in our own little world, that we fail to appreciate the wider picture. Prepare to have that tendency challenged…

The great gulf

Read Psalm 90

- ❓ *What does the psalm tell us about God?*
- ❓ *What does the psalm tell us about ourselves?*
- ❓ *What is the point of the contrast the writer draws between the two?*

One of the themes through Psalms 80-90 has been about the safest and best place to dwell. Here, we are reminded that God himself is our dwelling place. The safest place is in his arms, in his will. This is because when we dwell in God's presence, we are in the arms of the eternal God. His eternal dominion is in sharp contrast to our finite natures.

God existed before the world began. He is the one who created it. This doesn't just mean that his existence is stretched out over infinite years. God transcends and rules time so that "A thousand years … are like a day".

By contrast, our earthly existence is fleeting. God made our bodies from the dust and will return them to dust. We are fragile and frail; Ecclesiastes compares our life to vapour— a morning mist that quickly evaporates when the sun rises. We know that our life expectancy is around 70-80 years. So, the psalmist asks God to "Teach us to number our days" (v 12). In other words, we need to learn how to make the best use of our time.

This comes when we learn to fear God. It includes an awareness of his just anger, but it also requires us to fall upon the mercy and compassion of God. We number our days when we trust him and him alone to satisfy us.

☑ Apply

In a time when life expectancy has been growing, we can be tempted to act as though we are invincible and our lives will go on for ever. The reality is that our time here can end at any point through illness or accident. Even without those risks, our earthly lives are finite.

Take time to consider how you will make best use of your time. If you have 20 years of active service left, what do you want to do with it? What if you had only ten years to go? What would you prioritise? What will it mean for you to live this day as though it could be your last day?

☝ Pray

Ask God to help you to use the day ahead of you wisely and for his glory.

Pray that you would live today with the grand perspective in view—of God's greatness and your lowliness.

But rejoice that, despite this, his love for you is unfailing (v 14). Pray about this until you are satisfied, singing for joy and gladness.

GENESIS: Lot's line

We pick up the story in Genesis after the destruction of Sodom and Gomorrah. Lot's sad story continues in a downward direction.

At first glance, it is hard to find an edifying "thought for the day" from this particular Bible passage. But careful reading reveals something helpful...

Read Genesis 19:30-38

❓ *Why don't Lot and his family settle in Zoar, do you think?*

❓ *What is the girls' predicament?*

❓ *What verdict is given here on their "solution"?*

Lot and his daughters had just survived the equivalent of World War 3. Their home and region had been blasted to ash. Their wider family were all dead; their wife and mother had been calcified before their very eyes. It was likely that the locals were eyeing them with suspicion (v 30). They were reduced to living in a cave. But no rescuers were on the way, and no insurance payout was going to put them back on their feet.

The girls' situation was something like this: *Father is getting on. No one will have us. Here our family dies* (see v 31). The one desperate alternative which would keep the line of Lot alive was not, of course, one to which Lot himself would agree, and so they must ensure he knew nothing about it. Accordingly, they made him drunk—probably not difficult with a shocked and depressed old man—(v 33a), and in that condition, on two separate nights, each daughter had sex with him (v 33b).

Scripture offers neither judgment nor condemnation, but in this account we see the moral ruin of a whole family—and the rot started when Lot chose to "live dangerously" among the pagans.

The names of the children probably gave the neighbours a sly laugh (see v 37-38)—"Moab" sounds like the Hebrew for "from Father", and "Ben-Ammi" = "son of my people". Their descendants, however, would turn out to be fierce enemies of Israel. Lot took a pragmatic but ultimately self-serving choice. His daughters are only doing the same. But from these choices came centuries of enmity for Lot's family line and the children of Abraham.

✔ Pray

Lot was blessed (because of Abraham) but he himself ultimately brought trouble to God's people. Our moral choices can affect more than our own lives. What legacy will you pass on in your family and in your church?

Pray for wisdom in the decisions you make now and their future consequences.

Abysmal

The story of Lot has been a sorry saga. But thank God for the great heroes of faith who never failed, right? That, at least, is how we might feel until we read Genesis 20.

The line of promise

Read Genesis 20

❓ *What was the last thing that God told Abraham about the promised son (Genesis 18:10)?*

❓ *How is God's promise to Abraham now threatened?*

❓ *Why does God intervene as he does (Genesis 20:3, 18)?*

Incredibly, Abraham botches it again! Once again (compare 12:10-20), the deception that Sarah is his sister separates Abraham from his wife (20:2). And far from being two isolated incidents, it seems this was a strategy that they regularly resorted to when meeting strangers (v 13). Perhaps the experience with Pharaoh suggested it could earn them unexpected cash bonuses (12:16)!

But now the conception of Isaac is imminent. If Abimelek sleeps with Sarah, the fatherhood of Isaac could be called into question. Little wonder then that God's confrontation of Abimelek is so drastic (20:3), and all births cease in Abimelek's household (v 18).

Pray

Abraham's cautious habit actually reflects a failure to trust God.

❓ *What similar habits of ungodly prudence do you fall into?*

Ask God to help you give them up.

Grace abounding

❓ *Why does Abimelek stay innocent?*

❓ *What must he do to be restored after God's judgment on his household?*

God intervenes to keep Abimelek innocent by warning him in a dream of Sarah's true identity (v 3-6). Yet even a clean conscience cannot keep us out of trouble. Abimelek has unwittingly sailed into dangerous waters, but he must follow God's instructions to escape (v 7). And although Abraham has acted without any integrity or concern for Abimelek's innocence, still, as God's covenant-bearer, he is the one who must intercede for God's mercy on Abimelek's behalf.

It is Abimelek who emerges with honour, giving massive gifts to Abraham which confirm Sarah's innocence (v 14-16). Abraham compares badly. But once again, we see how God's covenant is one of total grace.

An heir is born

At last we come to the long-awaited event…

High point?
Read Genesis 21:1-7

❓ *What does verse 1 emphasise?*

The birth of Isaac should surely be presented as the high point of Abraham's story. And yet these verses are remarkably understated—just like the accounts of the resurrection! God is centre-stage here (v 1). He does for Sarah "what he had promised". There is no need for a great fanfare, as if it were remarkable that God does as he has said. What else would you expect?

❓ *Why, do you think, is the birth of Isaac described as what the Lord had promised to do for Sarah, rather than Abraham?*
❓ *What is Abraham's part in this event?*
❓ *How does the account underline that this birth is truly a miracle?*

Bearing the burden of the future

In spite of God's repeated, detailed promises to Abraham (12:2; 13:16; 15:4; 17:6), the focus here falls on Sarah, for, at this point, it is Sarah who must literally "bear" the burden. But Abraham is the one who officially names his son with the name given by God (17:19)—Isaac (= "he laughs"). And it's Abraham who, in line with God's earlier instruction (17:12), circumcises Isaac (21:4). Abraham's age, mentioned in verse 5, reminds us that this is indeed a miracle—as

much as creation or even the resurrection (see Romans 4:17).

For Abraham and Sarah this is a moment of pure joy—particularly for Sarah, whose "laughing boy" has at last given her something to smile about, but also for Abraham, who has received a gift beyond what anyone would have guessed. How often God exceeds what anyone would have believed.

✓ Apply

Abraham and Sarah's trust in God's promise was patchy—much like ours perhaps. But God's faithfulness to his own promises is never in doubt. Thank God for his faithfulness to Abraham and Sarah, which means that we can now enjoy salvation.

Read Romans 8:22-25 and be encouraged that patience in relation to the promises of our faithful God will always, finally, be rewarded.

Inheritance

Ah, the joys of family life! Martin Luther called married life a "school for character". For Abraham's family it is a very tough school indeed.

Family conflict

Read Genesis 21:8-14

❷ *In what way is Sarah right?*

❷ *In what way is she wrong?*

❷ *Why is Abraham less willing to agree with Sarah's demand this time (compare 16:1-6)?*

The joy following the birth of Isaac lasts only a year or so, until Isaac is weaned. Then Sarah's old wounds begin to fester. Sarah is right in her assertion that Ishmael will never share in Isaac's inheritance of God's covenant promises. However, it is meant as a statement of hostility in response to Ishmael's "persecution" of Isaac (see Galatians 4:29). Sarah's attitude here is far from exemplary and not at all the calm trust in God's faithfulness to his promises that we might expect.

⌄ Apply

Sarah's earlier actions (Genesis 16:2) left a legacy of bad feeling which has persisted until now. Her answer is to drive out the "cause" of the problem, regardless of the cost to the people involved.

❷ *What legacies of past failings still haunt you?*

❷ *How could you avoid following Sarah's example here?*

Family therapy?

Unlike previously, Abraham is distressed by his wife's demand (compare 16:2b). Ishmael is, after all, also his son (21:11). However, God reassures Abraham that he should indeed do what Sarah says, so as to secure Isaac's inheritance (v 12). God himself will take care of Ishmael (v 13). So Abraham sends Hagar off the next day (v 14).

Read Genesis 21:15-21

❷ *Why does God hear "the boy crying"— rather than Hagar—do you think?*

❷ *Why is God gracious to Ishmael and Hagar?*

God is not ignoring Hagar (see 16:7), but the emphasis here is on the link with Abraham (see 21:13). Ishmael is rescued to pursue a life separate from Abraham's line (v 21), but God is with him as he promised.

⌃ Pray

Pray for families in strife, especially those in your own church.

And pray that in times of stress and division between you and your family members, you would pursue what makes for peace.

Well hard!

Abraham's family line is at last secure and he is personally prosperous. He has also demonstrated the ability to hold his own in a fight. He is a force to be reckoned with.

Read Genesis 21:22-34

❷ *What is the purpose of Abimelek's visit?*

❷ *How do you think his previous encounter with Abraham (chapter 20) has influenced his attitude to Abraham now?*

❷ *And how do you think it has influenced Abraham's attitude to Abimelek?*

Abimelek is himself a God-fearer (see 20:3-7), and he sees that God is with Abraham (21:22). Abraham's false dealings with him nearly brought him to ruin. Although Abraham appears to have no stake in the land, Abimelek wants Abraham to swear on oath before God that he will treat Abimelek as generously as Abimelek once treated him (v 23).

Not surprisingly, and especially given the bad conscience he must have had, Abraham quickly agrees (v 24).

Water fight

Events, however, soon put this to the test. Water then was like oil today, a scarce resource which could easily become a focus of conflict. And that's what erupts over a well Abraham had previously dug (v 30). Abimelek's servants seize the well and Abraham complains (v 25). We do not know, and nor could Abraham, if Abimelek spoke the truth (v 26). But in the light of his earlier actions, Abraham was in no position to stand on his dignity. If the affair was to be settled

peacefully, a peace gesture had to be made. So Abraham made a covenant with Abimelek and handed over gifts (v 27) to validate his ownership of the well (v 28-30).

As God's people we live in the real world. This may mean being prepared to meet others halfway, and not always "standing on principle".

☑ Apply

❷ *When might it be "better" for God's people to be defrauded? See, for example, 1 Corinthians 6:1-7.*

❷ *Are there any circumstances in the past when you have unhelpfully stood on what you thought was a principle? What might you have done differently with hindsight?*

⌃ Pray

Pray for tact and diplomacy in dealing with others, especially when you are right.

The test

Child sacrifice was not an unusual feature of the religions of the ancient near east. Still, God's clear command must have come as a shock to Abraham...

Sacrifice

Read Genesis 22:1-14

❷ *What do God's words emphasise, as he instructs Abraham to sacrifice Isaac (v 2)?*

❷ *Find the signs of Abraham's calm trust that God would work it all out.*
- *v 5:*
- *v 8:*

❷ *What do you think was the basis for Abraham's trust?*

❷ *What does it mean to "fear God" (v 12)?*

God's command to sacrifice Isaac must have been a shock to Abraham after all the years of hearing God's promise and waiting for his son's birth. Even God mentions Abraham's love for Isaac (v 2). And yet there are no complaints, no questions, no delays, no alternative plans. Instead, the very next day Abraham sets out with Isaac and two servants (v 3). And when he leaves the servants so that he can go on alone with Isaac, he tells them, significantly, that "we" will return (v 5).

When Isaac notices that they lack the customary lamb (v 7), Abraham shows his trust in God to provide (v 8). He reasoned that ultimately God would keep Isaac safe so that his promises to Abraham wouldn't fail (Hebrews 11:19). And so it turned out.

The story confirms Abraham's fear of the Lord (Genesis 22:12), and also the grace and faithfulness of God. And it sets a precedent for the future: "On the mountain of the Lᴏʀᴅ it will be provided". This place, Mount Moriah, would become the temple mount in Jerusalem (2 Chronicles 3:1)—a picture of Jesus' redeeming work (John 2:19-22), just as the sacrificial lamb was a picture of him (1 Peter 1:18-19).

The demand for sacrifice, and its provision by God, go hand in hand. This is what trusting God is all about—obeying his word even when it will cut us deeply, and seems crazy from our limited viewpoint. This is the "work" that shows that faith is real.

···· **TIME OUT** ·································

Read James 2:20-23

❷ *What commands from the Lord do you find particularly difficult to take on board?*

🔼 Pray

Ask God to give you faith like Abraham's and an obedience that is unquestioning and uncomplaining.

Thank God, who has not held back his own Son so that we could be forgiven.

Emergency services

You have a nasty accident, you're threatened by someone, a fire breaks out. What do you do? You reach for the phone, dial the emergency number and ask for help.

Some situations are far more scary than those above, and which the fire brigade is unable to help you deal with .

Where do we dwell?

Read Psalm 91:1

What better security can there be? Like a ship safe in harbour during a storm, we dwell in the shelter of the Most High. Like someone sheltering under a tree from the intense heat of the sun, we rest in the shadow of none other than the Almighty.

> ❷ *When are you most prone to forget the protection of God?*

What will we say?

Read Psalm 91:2

When trouble comes, the writer openly expresses his trust in the Lord. Easier even than dialling the emergency services, we simply put our trust in the one who is our refuge and fortress.

> ❷ *Think about what you have planned for the coming week. When will you most need to remember to say this?*

What will God do?

Read Psalm 91:3-16

The psalm becomes more personal in v 3: "Surely he will save *you*".

> ❷ *In the final three verses, God is the one doing the speaking. I found eight things he promises to his people—can you find them all?*

⌄ Apply

Of all the promises in verse 3-13, pick the three you find most relevant. Rephrase them to reflect the dangers you will face this week.

1.

2.

3.

⌃ Pray

You may not be in any physical danger at the moment, but there are plenty of God's people around the world who are. It is estimated that, on average, over 300 believers die for their faith each day.

Pray for your persecuted brothers and sisters throughout the world. Ask that they might rejoice in the truth of this psalm.

Son of promise

In response to the tense climax of this mountain-top moment, God once again restates his promise to Abraham. Obedience leads to blessing...

....

Read Genesis 22:15-24

These few verses provide a crucial verdict on Abraham, and echo earlier affirmations of God's promises.

- ❷ *What's new about God's restatement of his promise in verses 16-17?*
- ❷ *Why does God take this further step?*
- ❷ *What is meant by "your only son" (v 2, 16, 12)? What about Ishmael?*

God adds to his promises by making an oath. Lacking anything greater to swear by, God confirms his covenant with Abraham by swearing by his own self (v 16). He does this to "make the unchanging nature of his purpose very clear" to Abraham and his descendants (see Hebrews 6:17).

God does this in response to the readiness of Abraham to offer his own, and only, son (Genesis 22:16). Here is an increasing spiral of grace... faith... obedience... greater grace... There is a link between God's grace and how his people live it out.

Which son?

Muslims claim that "your only son" (v 2, 12, 16) must refer to Ishmael, not Isaac. Isaac, they argue, was never Abraham's "only" son, whereas Ishmael was, at least for a while. But Ishmael is now out of the picture, not only physically, but also regarding the promise and inheritance (17:18-21; 21:14). Isaac is the only son of promise.

Earlier, God told Abraham to "keep the way of the LORD" (18:19; 17:1). In offering "his only son", Abraham was keeping "the way of the LORD". Surely, God himself would do no less than he demanded of Abraham. The ram (22:13) wasn't just a substitute for Isaac. Nor did it simply represent a future greater sacrifice *to* God, but one *by* God (see John 1:36)—of his "one and only Son" (John 3:16).

☑ Apply

God's grace and our response are connected. "Because you have done this" is not an empty phrase in Scripture.

- ❷ *How do grace and works relate to one another?*
- ❷ *Does obedience always result in blessing?*

Read Ephesians 2:8-10 and Hebrews 11:17-19.

☒ Pray

Praise God for the ultimate sacrifice, made for us in his Son.

And pray again for a determined obedience to the Lord's commands, whatever the circumstances, and whatever the potential outcome.

Love lost

The Bible draws a veil over what happens over the next several years. Then, inevitably, tragedy strikes.

Read Genesis 23

- ❓ *Where did Sarah die and where did Abraham bury her?*
- ❓ *Why do you think the purchase of Sarah's tomb is recorded in such detail?*
- ❓ *What is significant about Abraham's purchase?*

At the age of 127, Sarah breathes her last, and the depth of Abraham's loss is clear (v 2). This ancient couple, who have lived so many years together, and have been through so many hard times as well as good, are finally separated. Despite having been given the promise of land by God, this single purchase is the only land that Abraham possesses in his lifetime. But it is a seed that will grow.

▼ Apply

Some Bible commentators criticise Abraham for either too much or too little grief at the death of Sarah. But compare this with John 11:35 and 1 Thessalonians 4:13-18.

- ❓ *What perspectives does a godly attitude towards death and grief have that are missing from those who have no belief in God?*

Tomb talk

As anyone who has been bereaved will know, the practical details of the funeral must still be made, even in the midst of grief. So Abraham purchases a burial plot from the Hittites living in Canaan, in the customary Middle Eastern way (Genesis 23:3-16). The precisely detailed account of this makes it quite clear that this plot belonged to Abraham legally and completely—not stolen, or taken by conquest, but purchased by mutual agreement (v 20).

Heavenly hope

Abraham now owns the only piece of property which will ever be personally his in the promised land—a grave. Compare this with God's words to Abraham previously in 13:14-17. We might have expected Abraham's faith in the Lord to turn to disillusionment at this difficult time in his life, but it's not so.

- ❓ *How does Hebrews 11:8-10 explain the apparent discrepancy between the promise and its fulfilment?*
- ❓ *What are the lessons here for us?*

▲ Pray

- ❓ *How do you think you will cope with the death of someone close to you?*

How will you cope with the thought of your own coming death? By resting on the sure promises of God. **Read John 11:25-26.**

Pray for all those mourning the loss of someone dear to them.

The future

After Sarah's death, Abraham begins to think about finding a wife for Isaac, to whom God's covenant will pass.

Finding a wife
Read Genesis 24:1-9

❷ *Why did Abraham absolutely not want Isaac to marry a Canaanite (See 15:18-21)?*
❷ *Why might his servant fear that this was a "mission impossible" (Genesis 24:5-6)?*
❷ *What was the solution to the problem?*

Abraham knew that the Canaanites would one day come under God's judgment and be dispossessed from Canaan by his descendants. So he sent this trusted servant back to find a wife from his own people (v 4). But how to persuade a young girl to leave for ever her own land and people, and travel far and marry a man she knew nothing about from a family that she had never met? No wonder the servant raised the possibility of failure. But Abraham trusted that God would intervene to do what was necessary for his covenant to continue to the next generation (v 7), as the Lord had repeatedly promised to him.

⌄ Apply

Abraham doesn't wait for a wife to come to Isaac, but at the same time he's fully trusting that God is in control of what happens.

❷ *In what situations have you needed to take the initiative while also trusting God for the outcome?*

Passing the test
Read Genesis 24:10-27

❷ *How did the servant show himself worthy of Abraham's trust?*
❷ *What quality would his "test" reveal?*

On arrival, the servant matches Abraham's example by praying for specific guidance (v 12-14). Notice his wisdom—a girl who would perform her own tasks but also care for the needs of a stranger shows good character (see Proverbs 31:10-31). When Rebekah "passes the test" (Genesis 24:19-21), the servant makes his move. Rebekah's lineage (v 24) is the final confirmation that she is the one (v 26-27).

⌃ Pray

It's unwise to use this story as a strict pattern for marriage guidance. But it shows that God is sovereign in whatever happens (see 24:7-8).

Pray that you may know and do God's will right down to the details in your own life.

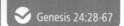

How to make a marriage

Finding a wife for Isaac involves some interesting bargaining, which may feel strange to some. But it is estimated that around half the world's marriages are arranged.

Bargaining for a bride
Read Genesis 24:28-50

- ❷ *What makes Laban so welcoming towards Abraham's servant (v 29-31)?*
- ❷ *What's the first thing that Abraham's servant tells Laban about his master (v 35-36)?*
- ❷ *What's the main point he gets across (see v 50)?*

Understandably Rebekah's brother takes a keen interest in Abraham's servant, but the gifts given to Rebekah make him curious, not hostile (v 31). The servant wisely begins his story with a description of Abraham's wealth—in other words, this is an arrangement that will be good for everyone (v 34-35). But he also explains how his quest is a divine mission under God's sovereignty (v 40, 42, 48). Laban and Bethuel seem to understand at least some of this—"this is from the LORD" (v 50). What God has purposed, they cannot oppose.

☑ Apply

Abraham's servant sees no contradiction between trusting God's sovereignty and making his case as persuasively as possible.

- ❷ *How is this also true of Christians, seeking to persuade unbelievers to turn to Christ? (See 1 Corinthians 9:19-22 and 2 Corinthians 2:14-17.)*

Love match
Read Genesis 24:51-67

More customs follow—gifts are given to Rebekah's family and etiquette requires an attempt to delay the return journey with Rebekah. In the end, things work out well, for Rebekah embraces the opportunity to marry Isaac and he is genuinely drawn to her (v 66-67).

☑ Apply

Neither arranged marriages nor love matches guarantee success—the future story of Isaac and Rebekah shows that. Marriages may be made in heaven but they require hard human work to keep them going.

- ❷ *If you are married, how is it going? Do you need to make more effort?*
- ❷ *If you are single, don't think that marriage is the end to all your problems; it is often just exchanging them for a set of new ones!*

☒ Pray

Pray for Christians starting out in married life, with all their hopes and fears, that they will stay faithful to God.

Judgment and grace

Abraham's story comes to an end. And yet it is not the end—because God's covenant promises will hold true for ever…

More wives

Read Genesis 25:1-11

❓ *How many more sons did Abraham have with Keturah?*

❓ *How did Abraham treat these sons? Why?*

This information about Abraham's family may surprise the first-time reader. Nothing else is said of this other wife, and yet, by the number of children she has (six in v 2), she and Abraham were together for some time. Abraham lived another 35 years after the marriage of Isaac (see v 7, 20), and he presumably married Keturah after Sarah's death. We also learn that Abraham had concubines.

Verses 3-4 tell us about the descendants of Abraham and Keturah. Could this be an outworking of the promise that Abraham's descendants would become as many as the stars in the sky? Abraham, however, was careful to put as much distance as possible between these later children and Isaac (v 5-6). These descendants were clearly not the fulfilment of the promise. That would only happen through Isaac and his descendants.

Funeral reconciliation?

❓ *How does the story of Abraham end in verse 11?*

Inevitably, we come to the death of Abraham himself (v 7-8), literally at a "good" old age, suggesting blessing to the last. Interestingly, both Isaac and Ishmael take responsibility for burying him—in the grave plot previously bought for Sarah (v 8-10). It's doubtful whether the brothers had been good friends while Abraham was alive. Indeed, earlier prophecy suggests Ishmael was a man of few friends (16:12). However, the death of their father seemed to bring about some sort of reconciliation.

Nevertheless, the story of Abraham ends with the specific note that it is Isaac who is blessed after his death (25:11), reminding us that the covenant has now passed to the son of promise. The book of Genesis will now focus on him.

🔼 Pray

Even the best life, lived under the hand of God, comes to an end.

Pray that you may learn, like Abraham, to obey God and to trust his sure promises.

And pray that you would live a life of significant service to God, and not retreat into self-serving comfort.

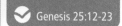
A house divided

The generational clock may have ticked onward, but the problems are very much the same: childlessness and strife.

Read Genesis 25:12-23

Ishmael

Once again, we have a genealogy—or rather two genealogies—of the descendants of Abraham. The first goes through the line of Ishmael.

- ❓ *What fact about Ishmael's origins are we reminded of in verse 12?*
- ❓ *Why, do you think?*
- ❓ *What's the main characteristic of Ishmael's line (v 18)?*

The mention of Ishmael's mother, Hagar the Egyptian, highlights Ishmael's significance—or rather his lack of it. Ishmael is prolific (a generation ahead of Isaac's line in producing twelve sons, v 14-16), but he hasn't inherited God's covenant with Abraham, and so the story of Abraham's descendants will move away from him. His only legacy to future generations is belligerence and strife (v 18).

🔼 Pray

The heartache of wayward children is a reality for many Christian parents. Pray for them, that they would continue to love and pray for their wandering children, and for the children to return to God.

Isaac

- ❓ *How is Isaac described?*
- ❓ *Why, do you think?*
- ❓ *How does the story of Isaac's family show God's sovereignty?*
  - *v 21:*
  - *v 23:*

Isaac is described simply as Abraham's son (v 19), not to ignore Sarah, but to underline the promise of God's covenant—the thing that matters most in this family history. From Isaac we move to Rebekah, and once again, there's the problem of barrenness. It seemed that Isaac had inherited his parents' fertility problems.

- ❓ *What was God teaching Isaac during those long years (v 21)?*

A comparison of v 20 with v 26 shows that it was 20 years before Isaac's prayer was answered! When pregnancy finally came about, it was Rebekah's turn to struggle and cry out to God. She learned the good news that from her womb would come not just twins but "two nations". The bad news was that they would be divided against one another—and shockingly, against all custom, the younger would be in charge!

But beneath this scandalous suggestion lies another "scandal"—the sovereignty of God in saving whoever he chooses.

Think about Paul's conclusion on this in **Romans 9:6-15**...

A Sunday song

We might imagine Old Testament Sabbaths to have been dreary days with lots of rules. But this "song for the Sabbath day" paints a very different picture.

Lips…

Read Psalm 92:1-4

- ❓ *What does the psalmist praise God for? And when does he do it (v 2)?*
- ❓ *How does praising God make him feel?*

☑ Apply

- ❓ *How's your singing in church? Do you share the psalmist's exuberant gladness? If not, why not?*
- ❓ *How can you increasingly make joyful praise your heart's beat from morning till night?*

☑ Pray

Spend some time now praising God for his love and his deeds. (If you have time, listen to a favourite song or sing a hymn.) If your spiritual life feels joyless at present, ask for God's help to be genuinely glad. Pray that your times of singing at church would stir your soul in praise of him.

… and lives

Read Psalm 92:5-15

- ❓ *What is it that "fools do not understand"?*
- ❓ *How does this psalm compare:*
  - *the way in which a wicked person "flourishes" (v 7) and a righteous person "flourishes" (v 12-13)?*
  - *God's status (v 8) and the writer's status (v 10)?*
  - *what happens to God's enemies (v 9) and the psalmist's enemies (v 11)?*

The final section of the psalm (v 10-15) is full of rich imagery. The horn is a symbol of power (v 10). The trees are meant to make us think of beauty and strength.

So how do we become majestic cedar trees, not withering grass? By planting ourselves in God's presence, and drawing nourishment from his word up through our roots (v 13). This is the secret to staying evergreen (v 14)! We can continue to bear spiritual fruit, even as our bodies age and slow down. In this way we proclaim God's greatness not just with our mouths, but with our very being. Our character testifies to God's character as much as our words do—we worship with our lives (v 14-15) as well as our lips (v 2).

- ❓ *Does this image of a flourishing tree remind you of any Christians you know?*
- ❓ *What is it about their character that is particularly beautiful?*

☑ Pray

Ask God to help you live out the truths you sing on a Sunday morning in the rest of the week. Pray that you would proclaim with your life and lips: "The Lord is upright; he is my Rock, and there is no wickedness in him".

Bible in a year: 1 Samuel 7-9 • Ephesians 5:1-16

The birthright

Isaac has prayed for children and God has promised that two nations will come from the twins that Rebekah will give birth to.

Read Genesis 25:24-28

❷ *How do you imagine Isaac's household—happy and harmonious, or mired in tension and conflict?*

❷ *What significant factors shaped Isaac's family?*

Isaac and Rebekah's twin boys are far from identical! One is red and hairy, prompting the name "Esau" (which vaguely resembles the word for "hairy"). Jacob's name carries the more negative sense of "dogging the heels" i.e. "seeking to overtake".

Not only are the two boys quite different in character but each is the favourite of one parent (v 28)—Esau, the "man's man" is doted on by his father, while Jacob is a mummy's boy in every sense. If the boys' different personalities could cause tensions, their parents' favouritism surely spells outright trouble!

The bargain

Read Genesis 25:29-34

❷ *What does this incident reveal about the characters of Esau and Jacob?*

Esau and Jacob were different in more than personality and interests. One evening, Esau returns tired and famished to find Jacob stirring a tasty-looking stew, and declares himself to be starving to death, though he recovers pretty quickly once he has eaten (v 34)!

Jacob also reveals his character at this point with his plain demand: "First sell me your birthright". This would have meant at the very least the headship of the family. And surely Jacob and Esau would also have known about the special relationship between their father and God. But instead of thinking of the future, Esau focuses only on the present (v 32) and Jacob gets the birthright.

⌃ Pray

Jacob was a cheat, but Esau was a fool. Neither is an example to follow!

Pray for wisdom to value God's gifts, and grace to resist temptations.

⌄ Apply

The New Testament comment is that Esau despised his birthright. It's easy to look down on Esau, but Christians are warned about falling prey to the same danger.

Read and reflect on **Hebrews 12:16-17**.

Bible in a year: 1 Samuel 10-12 • Ephesians 5:17-33

Trials and temptations

History appears to be repeating itself. But there is much more at stake here than a family's reputation and the happiness of a couple of people…

Action replay
Read Genesis 26:1-11

There are clear similarities between this story and that of Abram and Sarai in Genesis 12:10-20, but with a key difference.

- ❓ *What is 26:1 at pains to emphasise?*
- ❓ *What instruction from God does Isaac obey?*
- ❓ *Does obedience guarantee Isaac freedom from problems?*

Gerar was to the south-east of Gaza, and was evidently not a friendly place. Interest in Rebekah is understood by Isaac, as her husband, to potentially threaten his safety (v 7). On the other hand, every suitor knows the importance of being nice to a girl's brother! Unfortunately, Isaac gives the game away. When he thinks no one is looking, he enjoys a playful moment with Rebekah (v 8), and Abimelek the king instantly knows something is wrong (v 9).

- ❓ *What does Abimelek seem to have learned from his father (see 20:3-7)?*
- ❓ *What has Isaac not learned from his father's experience?*

⌃ Pray

- ❓ *What weaknesses (and strengths!) have you inherited from your parents?*
- ❓ *Ask God to help you learn from your family history…*

Reward
Read Genesis 26:12-22

- ❓ *Why does God choose to bless Isaac (v 12-14)?*
- ❓ *Does God's blessing guarantee Isaac freedom from problems?*

Isaac is blessed in accordance with God's promises—not because of anything he has done or not done (v 12-13). But notice that the outcome of God's blessing is more trouble—this time Philistine envy (v 14) and an attempt, literally, to block his progress (v 15). "Invited" to move away from Abimelek, Isaac has to keep moving until eventually he is far enough from the Philistines. The names of the wells tell the story—"Dispute" (v 20), "Opposition" (v 21), and only finally "Room" (v 22)—the Lord has given him room to flourish (v 22).

⌃ Pray

Despite Isaac's best efforts to botch everything up, God continues to protect, rescue and restore him. Amazingly, God's commitment to his covenant with this man overcomes all opposition and disobedience—even from Isaac himself!

- ❓ *Why is this an encouragement to us?*

Turn your answer into praise!

Alliances

Beersheba is a region (21:14), as well as the location of a well dug by Abraham (21:30-31). To this area Isaac now travels…

Read Genesis 26:23-25

❓ *What is God's purpose in appearing to Isaac there?*

❓ *For whose sake will God continue his covenant?*

Isaac's relationship with God is dependent on his own relationship with another—his father, Abraham (see 19:29).

⌃ Pray

This, of course, reflects the way our relationship with God depends on our relationship with Jesus.

Take time right now to praise God for providing Christ, and for all that Christ has made possible for us. (Read Ephesians 1:3-14 if you're stuck for something to say.)

Grace

Read Genesis 26:26-33

❓ *Why is Isaac suspicious of Abimelek?*

❓ *What is Abimelek's purpose in coming to Isaac?*

❓ *In what way is Abimelek being economical with the truth (v 29—compare v 16)?*

❓ *How does Isaac respond to Abimelek?*

❓ *How might he have been tempted to give a different response?*

Isaac wisely overlooks both the fact that Abimelek suddenly wants to be his friend,

and his disingenuous account of how Isaac was sent away. Instead, a meal is celebrated as the usual way of sealing a deal (v 30), and oaths are sworn (v 31). Abimelek shares in the blessing God has conferred on Isaac—another fulfilment of 12:3.

⌄ Apply

Read Romans 12:14-21

❓ *Where might you need to demonstrate Isaac's wisdom in overlooking rights and wrongs, and instead making peace?*

Grief

Read Genesis 26:35

❓ *Why were Esau's marriages in verse 34 doubly stupid?*

Not all alliances are equally good. Esau marries two women who are both foreigners—and so outsiders to God's covenant (compare Abraham, 24:3)—and a deep source of grief to his parents (26:35)! Once again Esau demonstrates his unsuitability to be the heir to the covenant.

⌃ Pray

Pray that you might make wise and godly decisions about when to build bridges and when to keep yourself "set apart".

Deception

Perhaps you struggle with feeling that you are not the right sort of person for God to choose. Perhaps you think you don't come from the right sort of family…

The plot

Read Genesis 27:1-29

❷ *What impression do you get of this family—of the individual characters and their relationships with one another?*

There's not much here to admire or imitate. Isaac still favours his eldest son. He is blind not only physically but also to the estrangements in his family. Rebekah uses Jacob's cause as a weapon in the power struggle against Isaac. She ends up cheating both her husband and her firstborn. Jacob goes along with his mother. We might feel sorry for Esau, but in the end he is reaping the consequences of his earlier disregard for his birthright.

Isaac's age and failing eyesight (v 1) prompt him to pass on the blessing of the covenant (v 4), but this also provides the opportunity for Rebekah and Jacob to deceive him.

❷ *How do you think God views Rebekah's scheme?*

❷ *What is God's plan for this family (compare 25:23)?*

···· **TIME OUT** ·······································

All this plotting to foil God's plans actually brings about God's plan.

❷ *Where else do we see this happen? Read Acts 4:23-28!*

❷ *Why does Jacob show reluctance (Genesis 27:11-12)?*

❷ *How does Rebekah persuade him?*

Jacob foresees problems (v 11-12). He's not troubled by moral scruples; he just doesn't want to get caught. But the issue is personal for Rebekah—she invokes the curse of her husband on herself (v 13). What resentments she must have accumulated over the years!

The blessing

❷ *How does the blessing reverse aspects of the curse given by God in Eden?*

❷ *How does Isaac try to reverse the prophecy given to Rebekah (25:23)?*

⌃ Pray

God chose Jacob over Esau, not because either was better than the other—they were both clearly awful, grasping and self-obsessed. He chose Jacob because he wanted to. Is that unfair? No, God is in charge. It's his decision to make.

Praise him that he has made that gracious decision for you too.

Remorse

Esau is about to discover the consequences of his frivolous attitude to his birthright. What he gave away many years ago has indeed gone from him.

Shock and awe

Read Genesis 27:30-40

- ❓ *What's the explanation for Isaac's violent shock (v 33) and Esau's extreme anguish (v 34 and v 38)?*
- ❓ *How does Isaac view the blessing he has just given Jacob (v 33)?*
- ❓ *Why does he struggle to find another blessing for Esau (v 37)?*
- ❓ *What's your impression of the blessing that Isaac finally gives Esau (v 39-40)?*

We are bound to feel sympathy for Isaac, an old man trembling with the shock of what he has inadvertently done to his firstborn—and for Esau, the brash and carefree hunter now reduced to terror and tears. Both of them know that the blessing cannot be revoked. "I blessed him," says Isaac, talking about Jacob, "and indeed he will be blessed".

All Esau can hope for is something at the bottom of the barrel (v 36). But Isaac has made Jacob Esau's lord and has ensured that Jacob will have all he needs (v 37). Even Isaac can see nothing left! The best he can manage, although called a "blessing", is little more than a curse (v 39-40).

☑ Apply

"Jacob I loved, but Esau I hated."

Read Romans 9:10-16

- ❓ *What lesson does the New Testament draw from this story about ourselves and about God's character?*

Problems

Isaac didn't intend to bless Jacob—he was deceived. So why couldn't the blessing be revoked? Surely it's because this deception coincided with God's plan—that Jacob, not Esau, should be the recipient of the covenant (Genesis 25:23). The blessing is not Isaac's in the sense of coming from him—it is only what he has received and must pass on. When it has gone to Jacob, Isaac no longer has control over it.

⌃ Pray

Life to carefree Esau must have seemed blessed until this fateful day.

Pray for a seriousness that will keep you from this kind of error.

Flight

Family fallouts are stock storylines in soap operas everywhere. It should be no surprise to us because such disagreements are both common and deeply dramatic.

The family fallout
Read Genesis 27:41-45

Although Esau's anger against Jacob might seem justifiable, the term for "grudge" (v 41) also appears in Psalm 55:3, describing the attitude of the wicked towards the man of God!

As Rebekah again intervenes to rescue Jacob, questions are raised about her marriage. She was hand-picked under God's guidance to be Isaac's wife (Genesis 24:12-14), something she herself consented to (24:57-58). We are even told that Isaac loved her (24:67).

❓ *Yet what impression do you get of Rebekah's character?*
❓ *What's the suggestion here about Isaac's character?*

Notice how Rebekah seizes control of the situation. Although everything works out according to God's intentions, it doesn't mean we should follow her example. However, Rebekah's scheming has been precipitated by Isaac's weakness—for his favourite son and his favourite food. If Isaac had paid proper attention to God's word (25:23), Rebekah would not have had to "take responsibility"!

🔼 Pray

At the very least, be warned that friction occurs even in the godliest of marriages.

Being at the centre of God's will does not automatically ensure that things will run smoothly.

Pray for Christian families and marriages that you know.

Continuing covenant
Read Genesis 27:46 – 28:9

❓ *How and why has Isaac's attitude to Jacob changed?*
❓ *What might lie behind Esau's attempt to please his parents(see Hebrews 12:17)?*

Isaac, now reconciled to God's purposes, willingly blesses Jacob in his quest for a wife—in fact, he reaffirms "the blessing given to Abraham" (Genesis 28:4).

By contrast, is Esau planning a way back into his father's affections (and perhaps his father's blessing?) by getting another wife? But with two wives of the "wrong sort" already (v 8), his latest marriage will hardly put things right at this stage!

···· **TIME OUT** ·································

Esau seems to keep believing he might patch things up. But actually he still refuses to take seriously God and his word.

Read Hebrews 12:17 and then compare with **1 Samuel 15:17-29**.

Mightier than the seas

Imagine an ocean—not the calm seaside scene of childhood summers, but the vast churning darkness of the mid-Atlantic. Keep that picture in mind as you read...

Read Psalm 93

The King's world

The first phrase in this psalm reads like an announcement: "The Lᴏʀᴅ reigns!" And this song begins a collection of psalms through to Psalm 100 that mostly focus on God as King.

- ❷ *What other words or phrases in this psalm emphasise God's kingship?*
- ❷ *What is it that guarantees the world's stability (v 1-2)?*

Verses 3-4 build up to a noisy crescendo. The roaring seas pitch and swirl; towering waves crash; the waters thunder—and yet the Lord is more powerful even than these.

⌄ Apply

- ❷ *In what way should this picture frighten us, do you think?*
- ❷ *In what way should this picture reassure us?*

God's power is terrifying—like a raging ocean he is big, dangerous and totally outside of our control. It's right to stop and stand in awe of him.

But if we're trusting in Christ, we do not need to be afraid. Jesus, who could silence the raging sea with a word, experienced the waves of God's wrath at our sin breaking over him on the cross. We can approach "the Lᴏʀᴅ on high" with calm—with awe-filled confidence rather than abject fear.

These verses carry great comfort for Christians. When the world seems out of control... when we feel under threat... when our personal circumstances are unsettled... this psalm reassures us: God is on our side, and he is mightier!

- ❷ *When might you need to remember that truth today? This week?*

The King's word

Just as God establishes the world, so he establishes his word (v 5).

- ❷ *What is truly beautiful (v 5)?*

God's house then was the temple (v 5).

Read 1 Corinthians 3:16-17

- ❷ *What is God's temple now?*
- ❷ *What does Psalm 93:5 tell us that the "temple" should be like? How long will it last?*

The psalm ends as it began—reflecting on God's unchanging permanence. God's word to his people is a solid rock—and by it, he shows us how to share in his beautiful holiness.

⌃ Pray

Spend some time worshipping God, the King who is robed in majesty.

The house of God

Jacob now sets out on his own—but he is not alone!

The place
Read Genesis 28:10-22

❷ *What does Jacob expect when he stops for the night?*

❷ *What is the significance of the stairway in his dream?*

Jacob stops at "a certain place" (v 11)—somewhere without apparent significance—simply because it is time to sleep. Jacob has not come to this place seeking God (v 16). What follows is all at God's initiative.

His vision is often referred to as "Jacob's Ladder", but it's really a stairway *from* earth *to* heaven on which angels are coming and going (v 12). More importantly, Jacob has an encounter with God (v 13).

···· **TIME OUT** ·······························

The stairway is a clear sign that our exclusion from Eden is reversible: but only at God's initiative. **Read John 1:51.**

❷ *How does Jesus fill in the detail of what Jacob's vision meant?*

The promises

❷ *What does the Lord God tell Jacob about...*
- *himself?*
- *the promised land?*
- *Jacob's descendants?*
- *world blessing?*
- *his relationship with his people?*

God has pronounced his covenantal blessing yet again to the next person in the chain of inheritance (compare Genesis 12:1-3 and 26:3-5).

The bargain
Re-read Genesis 28:16-22

❷ *In what way does Jacob wake up a changed man?*

❷ *List the various emotions that he displays.*

Notice that when Jacob wakes up, even the innocent camp site has become "awesome"—it is the place where heaven has met earth (v 17). To keep alive the memory of his encounter with God, he sets up a memorial and renames the place "house of God". He vows that if God will keep his promise, then he will be Jacob's God (v 20-21). It's not very profound, but it's heartfelt. Jacob now sees his life as resting in God's hands, and what he gets in future will be what he has received from God (v 22b).

◤ Pray

"Everything comes from you, and we have given you only what comes from your hand."
(1 Chronicles 29:14)

Like Jacob, recommit yourself to the God who cares for you.

Arrival

As Jacob nears Haran, he meets some shepherds who know Rebekah's family, and who identify for him Rebekah's niece—Rachel. Surely God is at work!

Seizing the opportunity
Read Genesis 29:1-14

❓ *According to Jacob, what should the shepherds be doing at this time of day (v 7)?*

❓ *What opportunity does their lazy attitude give to Jacob?*

Despite the hunger and thirst of their sheep, the shepherds are hanging about waiting for others to turn up (v 3, 8). It seems Rachel will be forced to wait with them out in the midday sun (see v 6 and 8). But her arrival gives Jacob a chance to show both initiative and strength. Single-handedly (and probably to the annoyance of the shepherds), he rolls away the stone and waters Laban's sheep (v 10).

Rachel tells her father, who immediately comes to greet Jacob. Doubtless Laban is already recalling what had happened with his sister (chapter 24). As Jacob had seized his opportunity, so Laban now seizes his.

🔽 Apply

God is about to start Jacob on a steep but valuable "learning curve". The trials he faces are perfectly designed by God to mould his character. It's the same for all who follow Christ.

❓ *Are you mature enough to understand that yet?*

Meeting his match
Read Genesis 29:14-30

❓ *Why do both Laban and Jacob think they are getting a good deal?*

❓ *Why does Laban get away with his fraud?*

❓ *What trouble will this episode store up for the future?*

Jacob is usually shrewd, but now he is also madly in love (v 18, 20). Seven years' work seems a reasonable price for Rachel as his bride. But the cheat is cheated! For a further price Jacob gets what he wants, but the curse of favouritism that has haunted Jacob's own family now threatens this new family unit (v 30).

🔼 Pray

Jacob's love for Rachel clouded his judgement. The Bible commends "levelheadedness" or "self-control" (e.g. Titus 2:2, 5, 6).

Pray for this quality in your own relationships and dealings with others.

The battle of the bulge

Many Bible characters practise polygamy. And each time, it records unflinchingly the pain, agony and dysfunction that results. God's original plan will always be the best…

Longing for love
Read Genesis 29:31 – 30:2

❷ *Identify the emotional state of each of the characters in this story. What drives their actions and dealings with each other?*
- *Leah:*
- *Rachel:*
- *Jacob:*

❷ *Why does God give Leah children?*

Jacob loves Rachel but not Leah. So God now acts with compassion for Leah, giving children to her rather than Rachel. The name of her first son expresses her longing for love: Reuben = "He sees my misery". But this longing (v 32) remains unfulfilled (v 33 and 34). After producing four sons Leah's fertility takes a pause—yet she has given birth not only to the eldest son but to men whose descendants will become priests (Levi) and kings (Judah). Meanwhile, Rachel's marital happiness and her relationship with Jacob suffer (30:1-2).

Longing for a child
Read Genesis 30:3-24

❷ *How does Rachel try to remedy her childlessness?*
❷ *How does Leah now treat Rachel (v 16)?*
❷ *What part does Jacob play in all this?*
❷ *Ultimately, what is the sole remedy for Rachel's childlessness?*

Meanwhile, desperation and insecurity bring out the worst in Rachel. Now begins "the Battle of all Mothers" with Jacob caught in the crossfire (v 1). Rachel's maidservant, as a surrogate mother, produces two sons for her. But Leah's counterattack equals the score. Rachel's next strategy involves an aphrodisiac (mandrakes bought from her sister for the price of allowing Leah a night with her own husband!). The result is success… for Leah, who conceives her fifth son. Rachel's infertility only ends when God gives her a son—Joseph.

And yet, despite the dismal wreckage of Jacob's fractured family, this is where God's salvation plan for the world is continuing to take shape.

⌃ Pray

This story highlights the deep distress suffered by those who are unloved and those who are childless. And how the family, designed by God as a place of comfort and support, can become a place of unhappiness because of bitterness and rivalry, or cowardly reluctance to get involved.

Pray for people struggling with natural longings that are unfulfilled. And for families embroiled in unhappiness and conflict.

Cheating the cheater

There's a certain soap-opera feel to this account of family feuding, manipulation and lying. Why exactly is this recorded for us in the Bible?

Exit strategy

Read Genesis 30:25-43

❓ *Why does Jacob want to leave (v 26, 29-30)?*
❓ *Why does Laban want Jacob to stay (v 27)?*

Jacob is still working for Laban and is past being ready to leave (v 25-26). But Laban has seen God at work in the fortunes of Abraham's line (v 27) and wants more of this blessing for himself. Jacob believes Laban has had enough "blessing" (v 29-30), and technically Jacob has already received his agreed "wages" in terms of his wives and children (v 26). Although Laban promises further wages (v 28), Jacob clearly mistrusts him. To get anything more, he needs to outwit his crafty employer.

❓ *Why do you think Laban agrees to Jacob's idea?*
❓ *How are Jacob's suspicions about Laban confirmed?*
❓ *Where does Jacob get his idea from (see 31:10-12)?*
❓ *What's the reason for Jacob's prosperity?*

Breeding bonanza

Jacob asks permission to keep the rarer-coloured animals of those he is tending, (30:31-33). Laban, seeing an obvious advantage for himself, agrees, but promptly removes this type from the flock, putting them out of reach (v 34- 36), thus increasing Jacob's disadvantage.

But Jacob's own scheme to outdo Laban involves a selective breeding programme, based on some genetic advice from an angel (31:10-12)! Despite Laban's precaution, Jacob's flock is still capable of bearing multi-coloured offspring. And by only breeding from the rarer and stronger animals, Jacob greatly increases his share of the flocks.

Jacob's breeding programme is based on the idea that what the animals see they will then produce. First, he puts striped branches in the watering troughs (30:37- 38); then he makes the "normal" animals face the rarer-coloured ones (v 40). It seems a successful strategy. But there's no link between what animals see and the offspring they produce. Jacob isn't blessed, nor is Laban thwarted, because of Jacob's efforts—the real reason for Jacob's prosperity becomes clearer later.

🔼 Pray

This story is not told to encourage trickery in our dealings with others. Rather, Scripture encourages us to deal with honesty and wisdom (see Colossians 3:22-25; Matthew 10:16). And yet we live in the real world, where such things are common.

Pray for honesty and wisdom in dealing with unscrupulous people.

Time to go

Envy can be a powerful force, and now it threatens to overwhelm Jacob and destroy him.

Estrangement
Read Genesis 31:1-16

> ❷ *What further tensions have surfaced in the family (see v 1, 2, 7, 15)?*
> ❷ *What is the real reason for Jacob's prosperity?*

It seems that Laban was not a good businessman (v 15), in spite of his schemes. He was not prospering like his son-in-law, and Laban's sons were blaming Jacob. Even Laban's daughters were feeling their father's growing hostility.

God's word confirms that it's time to go (v 3). But will Jacob return alone? Jacob explains to his wives that he is not simply running away, and he gives a detailed account of God's involvement—blessing him in spite of their father's worst efforts at cheating, and now "calling in" Jacob's vow made at Bethel (v 13). It suits Jacob not to admit to his own scheme to outwit Laban. Or perhaps he is realising what is already obvious to us—that God is the cause of his breeding success, not folklore remedies.

⌃ Pray

Jacob is slow in learning to trust in God, rather than his own schemes. But now it is God's word (v 13), rather than his own difficulties, which prompts Jacob to act.

Pray for patient trust in God's ability to bring about the right result without our "help".

Flight
Read Genesis 31:17-21

But Jacob isn't yet totally ready to give up his old scheming habits...

> ❷ *What scheme does he devise now?*
> ❷ *What does Rachel's theft reveal about this family?*

There's a rare agreement between Rachel and Leah. Their father's increasing hostility (v 14-15) persuades both of them to go with Jacob. But Jacob still can't trust in God to ensure that his instruction (v 13) is fulfilled, hence the secret departure.

As for the stolen idols, we might have expected Rachel (and Laban—see 30:30) to know better. Secret idolatry would remain a besetting problem in Jacob's household for centuries to come (see Joshua 24:23).

⌄ Apply

> ❷ *What family traits do you think you might have picked up and consider to be "normal"?*
> ❷ *How might you be nursing ungodly attitudes towards money, other people or success that might be considered wise in a worldly sense, but are not ultimately wise in a Christian sense?*

Read Colossians 3:1-10

Covenant

Laban responds with fury to Jacob's departure. But before he can act on his anger, God intervenes…

Rage and indignation
Read Genesis 31:22-35

The Hebrew in verse 24 can mean [say] "no word" or [do] "no thing". Since Laban eventually says quite a lot to Jacob, apparently he understood this warning to mean he should not harm Jacob (v 29).

Look at what Laban says to Jacob (v 26-30).

❷ *What do you think is fake, and what is genuine?*
❷ *What is Jacob's view of Laban and his speech?*

Jacob's response is the equivalent of "Yeah, right!" The extravagant send-off pictured in v 27-28 is totally unbelievable, while surely, Jacob thinks, the accusation of theft is just another of Laban's ruses to regain power over him—hence Jacob's strong protestation of innocence—and the fearsome vow he makes (v 32).

Jacob's righteous indignation is ironic. The deceiver has even managed to deceive himself into thinking he is innocent of plotting his escape And Rachel can match her father's cunning, pleading her period for not giving away where she has hidden the idols, so Jacob isn't cornered by his vow, and his family escapes disaster.

Reconciliation
Read Genesis 31:36-55

Jacob and Laban now have a frank exchange of views.

❷ *How has Laban harmed Jacob (v 36-42)?*
❷ *How has Jacob harmed Laban (v 43-44)?*
❷ *How does Jacob finish his speech (v 42)?*

Notice that Jacob's long list of complaints ends with a full and profound confession of his God, whom he refers to as "the Fear of Isaac"—a new and unique description of the Lord. It's as if Jacob suddenly discovers his faith as he blurts out this summary of the past two decades.

Laban also has his pain. He cannot keep his children, but he proposes a covenant between himself and Jacob (v 44)—a kind of reconciliation and also a guarantee of security for his daughters (v 49-50). But note that the reconciliation is a "patch-up job". Incomplete but not fully satisfying. This is the way life must be sometimes in our messy, sin-soaked world.

🔺 Pray

Both Laban and Jacob have caused each other pain. Reconciliation is the right outcome.

Pray for those whom you have hurt and offended, however innocent you may feel yourself to have been.

Does God really care?

In this psalm, God's people are under attack. And they are still today: Open Doors estimate that 322 Christians around the world are killed for their faith every month.

The charge
Read Psalm 94:1-7

- ❷ What does the writer ask God to do? Why?
- ❷ Can you think of places around the world, or incidents in the news, where God's people have been "crushed", "oppressed" or "murdered"?

The psalm acknowledges that God is "Judge of the earth", but the question of verse 3 is still anguished. The charge against God is that he "takes no notice" that people—even his own people—are suffering. Is that true? The rest of the psalm offers three responses.

Answer #1
Read Psalm 94:8-11

- ❷ What answer does verse 11 give to the questions in verses 9-10?

Answer #2
Read Psalm 94:12-15

- ❷ How does the writer describe "the one you discipline" (v 12)?

God uses hard times to mould our character to be more like Christ's (see Hebrews 12:7-11). This can be incredibly painful—but ultimately, it is the way to blessing.

Answer #3
Read Psalm 94:16-19

- ❷ How has the writer experienced God's personal care in dangerous times?
- ❷ Can you remember a difficult time when God's love supported you and brought you joy?

So does God see when his people are oppressed? Yes, he does. Is God at work through his people's suffering? Yes, he is. Does God care for his people in the midst of trouble? Yes, he does.

The conclusion
Read Psalm 94:20-23

God is not on the side of the corrupt (v 20). So although the wicked continue to attack the innocent (v 21), God will bring them to justice in the end (v 23). The New Testament reveals more about what God's judgment will look like. **Read 2 Thessalonians 1:5-10.**

The psalmist's plea for God's judgment in Psalm 94:1-3 has become a confident declaration (v 23). In verse 3 the writer cried, *How long?* In verse 23, he rests in the knowledge that God will judge.

The idea of God's judgment often makes us uncomfortable, especially when we think of people we love who don't trust Christ. But this week, in the world around you and in the news, look for reasons to view God's judgment with the psalmist's sense of relief.

Bible in a year: 2 Samuel 12-13 • 1 John 3

Tact and diplomacy

Jacob is returning to the land God has promised to Abraham and Isaac. But he must have had a sickening feeling as he returns to face another broken relationship.

Jacob's predicament

Read Genesis 32:1-21

The encounter with angels prompts Jacob to name the place where he enters the promised land "Two Camps". In effect, he's entering "divine territory".

❓ *How does this inspire his own plan to rescue his family from Esau (v 7-8)?*

Jacob now sends word of his return to his brother, Esau (v 3-4). He is conciliatory (v 5), but the response is terrifying (v 6). The 400 men coming with his brother (v 6) are clearly not a welcoming committee! Not surprisingly, Jacob throws himself on God in prayer, which, if not selfless, is heartfelt and truthful (v 9-12). Sometimes sheer terror can push us into the arms of God.

🔽 Apply

Jacob must at last face up to the unresolved problem of his brother. Many of us have "skeletons in the cupboard" which need to be brought out into the clear light of day.

❓ *Is there anything you need to talk to God about now?*

Jacob's prayer

❓ *Has Jacob's present crisis arisen out of obedience to God or disobedience? (v 9)?*
❓ *Why does he mention how unworthy he is of God's kindness (v 10)?*

❓ *What else does he mention (v 12)? Why?*

Jacob articulates three reasons why he trusts God to save him—God's command (to return to the promised land), God's mercy, and God's promise to preserve him and his descendants. Surely God will not allow his command to be prevented, his grace to be overcome or his promise to be broken.

Having prayed, Jacob sets aside a generous gift for Esau (v 13-15), but divides it into instalments (v 16-20), to create a good impression and also to wear down Esau's fury. Then Jacob is left alone for probably the longest, certainly the most significant night of his life...

🔼 Pray

Jacob prays best when in fear of his life. Surely this is one reason why God gives us such trials (see 2 Corinthians 1:3-7).

Give thanks to God that your troubles are personally designed by him to make you trust him more.

Wrestling with God

What follows is one of the most remarkable passages in Scripture. It's worth taking time to think carefully and openly about it, and reflecting on its meaning for us.

A new experience of God

Read Genesis 32:22-32

The events of Jacob's night alone are among the most extraordinary in the Bible. Until now he has been a "chancer", and God has been an adjunct to his life—yes, looking after him (31:5), yes, blessing him (31:9), even demanding his obedience (31:13). But somehow Jacob has never quite allowed God to have him.

❓ *Who is it that Jacob wrestles with (32:28, 30)?*

❓ *What's surprising about verse 25?*

❓ *What's surprising about verse 26?*

Jacob is now forced to confront God, as verse 30 makes clear—but this is no polite conversation with a "still, small voice of calm"! Instead, there is sweat, grunting, breathlessness, fear, anger, elation and exhaustion! Even more surprisingly, the "man" cannot overpower Jacob (v 25a) until a "special move" is put on him (v 25b). Finally, Jacob will not let go, insisting on a blessing first (v 26)!

⌄ Apply

Do we expect God always to pick us up when we fall, and cuddle us when we're distressed? This "motherly" view of God is not wholly wrong (see Isaiah 66:13). But here Jacob discovers a "fatherly" God, who tosses his children around and wrestles with them, even though, as Martin Luther acknowledged, "This playing means infinite grief and the greatest anguish of heart" at the time.

A new name

Jacob's new name, "Israel", means "he struggles with God". Compare the name of his great-uncle—"Ishmael" ("God hears you", Genesis 16:11). Jacob's name seems more appropriate to the sceptic and the unbeliever, yet he is the one God blesses (32:29b).

Jacob is never the same again after this spiritual smackdown. God has touched him, not to heal, but to hurt (v 31)! Yet through that hurt, Jacob is made whole.

⌃ Pray

Having faith does not mean lacking struggles. It can be an expression of faith to struggle with God. It's not wrong to "wrestle back" when God seems to make things difficult (see Psalms 38 and 88).

❓ *Is there anything that you want to say to God right now?*

Reunion

Freshly crippled by God, Jacob must face the trial that has been terrifying him for so long; meeting the brother he robbed of everything—Esau…

Reconciliation
Read Genesis 33:1-11

> ❷ *How do you think Jacob feels as he finally approaches Esau?*
> ❷ *What suggests that Esau has already been won over?*
> ❷ *What is Jacob's attitude to Esau?*

Despite his encounter with God, Jacob clearly still fears meeting Esau. In one last defensive stratagem he divides his family, putting Rachel furthest from trouble at the back, but taking the front himself.

But Esau has apparently already been won over. His emotional welcome (v 4), his eagerness to catch up on the family news (v 5), even perhaps his attempt to decline Jacob's gift of animals (v 9)—all suggest a genuine desire for reconciliation on Esau's part. Jacob too seems keen to win Esau's favour (v 8b, 10-11), and he persuades Esau to take the gift, underlining the reconciliation between the two brothers.

✓ Apply

Broken relationships run deep—especially when they are family relationships. Reconciliation is never easy. Pray for those who need to be reconciled in your fellowship—perhaps that includes you!

Ask God for a spirit of humility and a desire for "one-ness" in Christ.

Retreat
Read Genesis 33:12-20

> ❷ *Why do you think Jacob leaves Esau?*

The reconciliation is not perfect. Perhaps Jacob fears Esau will change his mind. Maybe a bad conscience means he finds his brother's company uncomfortable. Whatever the reason, old habits of deceit die hard, even for a renewed man of God. Despite what he has said to Esau (v 14), Jacob heads in a different direction.

Finally in the promised land, Jacob builds an altar to "God, the God of Israel". The God of Abraham and Isaac is now the covenant God of Jacob (or "Israel").

✓ Apply

By God's grace Jacob has survived many dangers, yet he is still unwilling to trust God fully.

> ❷ *Does this ring any bells with you?*

⌃ Pray

Like Jacob, each of us has some besetting weakness that we will continually have to struggle against even as we grow in our faith.

Speak to the Lord about that now, and claim the promise of 1 John 1 v 8-9.

Like father... like son

Arrival in the promised land is no guarantee of a problem-free life for Jacob...

Attempted restitution?

Read Genesis 34:1-24

Shechem's rape of Dinah (v 2) is not excused by the fact that he falls in love with her (v 3, 19). Verse 7 emphasises that this is a disgraceful thing.

- ❷ *What's attractive about Hamor's proposal for Jacob and his family (v 8-12)?*
- ❷ *Why is it attractive to the Shechemites (v 23)?*
- ❷ *What's the danger for Jacob's family? (Compare Genesis 24:3-4; 26:34-35; 27:46 – 28:2.)*

Hamor, wishing to make amends for his son's behaviour and to legitimise the relationship (34:6, 8-10), suggests an alliance between the two families that could lead to increased prosperity all round (v 9-10). Privately, however, the Shechemites are confident that the newcomers will be subsumed by themselves (v 23). There's a real danger that Jacob's family will disappear into the surrounding Canaanite community. Nevertheless, Jacob appears willing to go along with Hamor's plan, since he does not immediately rally his own sons (v 5).

An act of revenge

Read Genesis 34:25-31

- ❷ *What motivates Jacob's sons?*
- ❷ *What is Jacob's concern?*

- ❷ *What perspective do both Jacob and his sons lack?*
- ❷ *How is God's sovereignty at work here?*

Jacob's sons have learned well from their father! Their insistence on circumcision is a deceit designed to lure the enemy into weakness (v 13-15). The result is that, contrary to the Shechemites' hopes, everything goes to Jacob's family.

Jacob's sons are motivated by revenge (notice how utterly disproportionate their violence is, v 25-29). Jacob is again stricken by fear (v 30). No one seems either concerned for, or confident in, the covenant promises of God to their family. But... although there's little godliness here, and Hamor's proposal and Jacob's acquiescence would have threatened the future of God's people, God graciously works within this sinful situation.

☑ Apply

Understanding God's sovereignty and grace gives us confidence that even in what looks like catastrophe, God is still working.

- ❷ *Are there personal situations that you are involved in that need this understanding applied to them?*

Full circle

For many years Jacob had been away from the land, and distant from the promises and revealed plan of God for the future. At last he returns...

Break with the past

Read Genesis 35:1-8

❓ *Why do you think God wanted Jacob to build an altar at Bethel (see v 1, 7; but compare 28:10-22)?*

❓ *What was Jacob's family like spiritually at this stage (35:2)?*

❓ *How did they mark a break with the past (v 4)?*

Jacob's life is about to come full circle (v 1). Bethel had been his point of flight from the land of promise (28:10-22), so this return marks an end to his wanderings. The specific instruction to build an altar underlines the spiritual nature of this return.

Surprisingly, you may think, idolatry was rife in Jacob's family (35:2)—it seems that Rachel was not the only one carrying "foreign gods" around. So Jacob sought to cleanse his family. Washing, clean clothes (compare Exodus 19:10) and burial at Shechem of all the tokens of their former beliefs and loyalties were all ways in which they marked a break with the past.

❯ Apply

Read 1 John 5:18-21. Christians who know the truths that John highlights here still need his final warning: *"Dear children, keep yourselves from idols"*. Ask God to help you identify idols that still tug at your heart, and to show you how to leave them for ever.

Arrival

At Bethel, Jacob carried out God's instructions, building the altar and rededicating the site to "El Bethel" ("The God of Bethel"). Bethel was where God had revealed himself to Jacob—where their relationship could be said to have truly begun, where God had graciously answered an undeserving Jacob "in the day of [his] distress" (Genesis 35:3) and had blessed him ever since. To Jacob, Bethel was a place of promise and hope. But notice it was also to become a place of sadness (v 8).

❯ Apply

The kingdom of God has been helpfully described as "God's people, in God's place, under God's rule". This could describe Jacob at Bethel. But great though the blessing is, this is not the end of the curse—there is still weeping and death (v 8).

Believers have a vision of perfection in the Lord Jesus, in Eden and in the new creation. But we cannot mistake what is to come with what can be achieved here and now.

❓ *How can you fight the disillusionment and disappointment of living in a fallen world?*

Renewing the covenant

It is truly remarkable how many personal encounters with God Jacob had—and all the while he remained a flawed, cheating, unreliable man. Grace in action.

Read Genesis 35:9-15

These verses begin: "After Jacob returned from Paddan Aram"—something that had actually taken place several years earlier (see Genesis 31:17-21). The wording of 35:9 makes a leap from the time Jacob left Laban to the time of his return to Bethel. The significance of what happens here at Bethel outweighs all that went on during the intervening period. What follows is what really counts!

🔼 Pray

God's hand is on all our days, but certain points in our lives seem to matter more than others. Years of profitable ministry and being used by God may flow from a single decision. Similarly, years of profitable ministry may be undone in an unguarded moment.

> ❷ *Is there a crucial decision to be made today? Ask God to keep his hand upon you as you make it...*

Blessing

> ❷ *What three things does God confirm?*
> - *35:10 (compare 32:28)*
> - *35:11a (compare 1:28)*
> - *35:11b-12 (compare 17:6, 8)*
> ❷ *How does God want to be known by Jacob? See 35:11 (compare 32:29).*

At Bethel, God appears to Jacob for the third time and blesses him. He confirms the new name by which Jacob is to be known, following the wrestling incident at the Jabbok (35:10, compare 32:24-28). God now reiterates the creation blessing given to Adam and Eve (1:28). But Jacob also inherits the blessing of Abraham—to be the father of many nations and kings (35:11), and the promise of the land (v 12).

God also reveals himself further through his own self-naming: "God Almighty" (*El-Shaddai*, v 11a), reminding Jacob that the God with whom he struggled cannot be overcome—"Almighty"—and yet he does not denounce our struggles with him!

🔼 Pray

Take some time to review what has happened since God confirmed to Isaac his promises to Abraham (26:2-5).

> ❷ *What problems and dangers have threatened the family that bears his covenant?*

Praise God that, despite the sin of his people and the enmity of others, his covenant promises remain on track. Truly he has proved himself to be "Almighty".

Careful how you hear

Listening to God's voice is a very, very dangerous thing to do...

Worshipped

Read Psalm 95:1-7a

❷ *What does the psalmist call on God's people to do, and why:*
- *in v 1-2 and 3-5?*
- *in v 6-7?*

The creation we see around us was sculpted by God's hand, and is held in God's hand. The only fitting response is to worship him, humbly and joyfully accepting the loving care of this Good Shepherd (v 6-7).

But in the second half of the psalm, there's an unexpected twist. The psalmist wants to warn us that there is a very real possibility of us rejecting this Shepherd-King.

Rejected

Read Psalm 95:7b-11

To understand these verses, we must travel backwards, then forwards, in Bible history.

Read Exodus 17:1-7

❷ *Why is the Israelites' complaint in verse 3 utterly ridiculous?*

The Israelites "tested" God at Massah; they refused to take him at his word—to trust that he would do what he had said he would do. Hearing without believing, listening without trusting, is deadly. And this was no one-off incident; it was a repeated pattern, stemming from a hard, unbelieving atti-tude. So God delayed the Israelites' arrival

in the promised land for 40 years (Psalm 95:10-11). But it's not just the Israelites who are at risk...

Read Hebrews 3:12-15; 4:8-11

"Today", on Sunday 5th November 2023, God is offering you "rest": salvation. He grants us a "share" in Christ's righteousness (3:14). So we can stop striving to earn his acceptance, and instead "rest"—both now and in eternity—because Christ has done everything needed.

❷ *How does Hebrews 3:12-15 show us more of what it means to "harden [our] hearts"?*
❷ *What are we told to do to avoid this happening (v 13)?*

✓ Apply

❷ *Who could you encourage today? How might you do that, considering what these verses say?*
❷ *How can you make sure you get this daily dose of protection against sin's deceitfulness?*

If these verses leave you feeling fearful, ask yourself, am I trusting in Christ today? If the answer is yes, then "sing for joy" (Psalm 95:1-2)! After all, it's as we give thanks for what God has done for us through Christ that we are compelled to bow before him (v 6). And sin's deceitfulness looks a lot less attractive as we look up from the feet of our Good Shepherd.

A death in the family

Jacob's return to Bethel, and the confirmation of God's covenant blessing, could be seen to mark the highlight of his life. Surely, from this point on, all will be plain sailing…

Read Genesis 35:16-29

- ❷ *In what ways does Jacob's life take a turn for the worse?*
- ❷ *What has been Rachel's greatest longing (see 30:24)?*
- ❷ *What can we learn from its fulfilment and the consequences?*

Nemesis

Rachel named her only son Joseph in the hope that God would add another son to her tally (30:24). But the arrival of the hoped-for son proves to be her nemesis, for she dies in childbirth. Rachel calls him "son of my trouble" (35:18a). It's a terrible name to carry through life, so Jacob calls him "son of my right hand" (18b)—"Benjamin".

⌄ Apply

The fulfilment of Rachel's greatest longing turned out very differently from what she must have imagined. The lesson here for us is that all the pleasures, achievements and experiences of this life—all blessings from God himself—are contaminated by the corruption of sin, decay and death.

Take to heart the words of **Ecclesiastes 9:7-9** and **Matthew 6:19-21**.

Rivalry

And there's more trouble. Jacob's eldest son has sex with Jacob's concubine—an act which was, in effect, a takeover-bid for power in the family. The verdict on this betrayal will come at the end of Jacob's own life (see Genesis 49:3-4). But at this point the family is complete in number, and there is a "roll call" of Jacob's children (35:22-26).

Finally, Jacob returns to Isaac who, contrary to expectations (see 27:2), has lived to greet his son's return (35:27). Soon after, however, Isaac dies.

- ❷ *What does verse 29 remind you of (compare 25:7-9)?*
- ❷ *Remember the pattern of Genesis 5? How much has really changed since then?*

Another generation passes on. God's covenant with Abraham is taking shape, yet God's curse on Adam remains.

⌃ Pray

Pray for families where godly members are seeking to cope with ungodly relatives.

Summing up

This chapter clears the ground for the final section of the book. It details the family line of Esau, who is now to fade into the background.

However, the nation of Edom (another name for Esau) will remain a significant but unwelcome force in the history of Israel.

Families matter

Read Genesis 36:1-19

❓ *What failing of Esau's are we reminded of in verses 2-4 (compare 26:34)?*

❓ *What reason is given for Esau's distance from Jacob?*

❓ *What other factors were likely to produce this distance between the brothers?*

❓ *What's the overall impression we get of Esau's family?*

One of Esau's several mistakes was his choice of wives, who were Canaanite and Ishmaelite (36:2-3). Note that verses 2-3 differ from the earlier accounts of Esau's wives in 26:34 and 28:9—possibly these were alternative names, just as Esau was also known as Edom.

Never underestimate the power of marital allegiance! Esau's family connections meant there was little hope of harmony with Israel's descendants. Esau's family was large and prosperous like Jacob's (36:6-7), but the distance between them was more than physical—spiritually, they had also taken completely different directions.

TIME OUT

The details of Esau's family, although of little long-term interest to us, are presented as an accurate record. This is not "myths and legends", but a verifiable (back then, anyway) account of historic events.

Read Genesis 36:20-43

The Horites, whose family is listed in verses 20-30, were to be dispossessed by the Edomites (see Deuteronomy 2:12). Esau married into the family via the daughter of Anah, son of Zibeon (compare Genesis 36:24 with v 2). "Hivite" (v 2) and "Horite" (v 20) seem to be interchangeable names.

The Edomite kings (v 31-39) didn't seem to inherit the monarchy from each other—perhaps they were elected...

Pray

So near to, and yet so far from God's work through Jacob—powerful, prosperous Esau was sidelined by unfaithfulness.

Pray for people you know who are so near to and yet so far from salvation.

1 JOHN: We know…

Welcome to 1 John. Today, we're going to scan through the whole letter, picking up its main themes.

The sender

Read 1 John 1:1-3

We'll look at these verses in more detail to-morrow. For now, although the early church and the style of the letter both make clear that the author is the apostle John, notice that the sender doesn't identify himself by name. Instead, he gives us his credentials for writing…

- ❷ *What does he say about his relationship with "the Word of life"?*
- ❷ *Why should this make us excited, and humble, as we read 1 John?*

The message

Read 1 John 2:5b-6

- ❷ *How do we know we are really Christians?*

Read 1 John 3:16

- ❷ *How do we know what love is?*
- ❷ *How do we show that we know what love is?*

"Brothers" (or "brothers and sisters", NIV2011) is John's way, throughout this let-ter, of saying, "Christians". In other words, we show that we are loved by Christ in how we treat our brothers in Christ. We show that we live in Christ by living like Christ. So 1 John is all about reminding us of how God has loved us in Jesus, his Son, and exhorting us to live that out in our lives.

The threat

In this sense, 1 John is a wonderfully encouraging letter. But all was not well among the first readers…

Read 1 John 2:18-19, 22-23, 26

"Many antichrists have come"—many people whose teaching opposes the truth about Christ.

- ❷ *What kind of things do these people seem to have been saying (v 22-23)?*
- ❷ *What was the danger to the true Christians (v 26)?*

So here's 1 John in a nutshell: *we know we know Christ if we are seeking to live like Christ and hold to the truth about Christ.*

···· **TIME OUT** ··

- ❷ *When do you find yourself doubting what the Bible says about Jesus?*
- ❷ *When do you find it hard to live as Jesus says?*

Those are probably the areas of your life you can expect 1 John to be speaking to as we go through this letter!

▲ Pray

Pray now for a mind that understands 1 John, a heart that is willing to be challenged by 1 John, and a life that will be transformed by 1 John.

Why listen to John?

We live in a society increasingly suspicious of authority. Media, police, politicians, ministers… You can't seem to trust them! So why should we trust John?

Alongside this, we live in a society increasingly deluged by information. Twitter, Facebook, online books… There's too much! So why should we make time to listen to John?

Life

Read 1 John 1:1-2

- ❓ *What are these verses "concerning"— what are they all about (end of v 1)?*
- ❓ *What is John "proclaim[ing]" about the Word of life (v 2)?*

Notice that "appeared" features twice here. Once it refers to "the life"—then to "the eternal life". In other words, a life was lived on earth that allows us to live eternally. When this man turned up, so did eternal life.

- ❓ *Why is John able to speak with confidence about the Word of life's appearance on earth (v 1)?*

Verse 1 is staggering, when we stop to reflect. Here is someone who "was from the beginning"—God—and yet someone who could be heard, seen, weighed up (which is the sense of "looked at") and touched. The infinite became finite. It is amazing.

···· **TIME OUT** ···

Read John (not 1 John!) 1:1-14

- ❓ *What similarities do you see between the opening of John's Gospel and the opening of 1 John?*

Community

John has authority to write because he is writing about what he has seen and heard. John deserves our attention because he's writing about the life that brought eternal life. And that's not all…

Read 1 John 1:3-4

- ❓ *John proclaims what he's seen so that… What (v 3)?*
- ❓ *And he writes this down in order to… What (v 4)?*

Humanity was built for community. Community with each other, in love and harmony, is what the church is (or is meant to be). But even more than that, we were made for community with the God of community— God the Father, his Son, Jesus, and the Spirit. And not simply a functional community but a joyful community (v 4). John could have simply said, *We proclaim salvation.* But he wants to show us that we are saved to be in community with our God and his people, and that we are saved to know joy—a joy we find in that community.

☑ Apply

- ❓ *Do you find your greatest joy in community with God and his people? How does this express itself?*
- ❓ *How do these verses give us confidence that 1 John will be able to help us to hold to the truth about Christ?*

Fake news industry

We've seen that there were people who were "trying to lead [the Christians] astray" (2:26). Here, John makes one statement and then opposes three false teachings.

Read 1 John 1:5

❓ *What does John state about God?*

Totally pure, utterly perfect, dazzlingly holy. That's the real God. And if we know him, three views are ruled out for us...

Wrong view #1

Read 1 John 1:6-7

We can claim to be Christians all we like...

❓ *But what would show that we aren't really Christians (v 6)?*

If you're in close relationship with someone, you live close to them (emotionally, if not spatially). God is "light"; so, if you deliberately live in darkness, you're not close to him.

❓ *What happens if we do seek to live pure lives, in the "light" (v 7)?*

John isn't saying we must be perfect (or we wouldn't need purifying from sin). He's calling us to be committed to pursuing purity.

Wrong view #2

Read 1 John 1:8-9

Being "without sin" = saying, "I'm not really a sinner".

❓ *If we claim this, what do we do (v 8)?*
❓ *What is the opposite of claiming to be without sin (v 9)?*

This is challenging. If we're not people who deliberately, regularly confess our sins to God, we're closet sinfulness-deniers.

❓ *What happens if we do confess (v 9)?*

Wrong view #3

Read 1 John 1:10 – 2:2

This seems to be about particular sins— making excuses for them, belittling their seriousness or denying they're sinful at all.

❓ *Whenever we do this, what are we saying about God (1:10)? About ourselves?*
❓ *We shouldn't sin—but if we do, what do we know (2:1-2)?*

We don't need to excuse or cover up our sin. We can confess, knowing that Jesus is saying to his Father, *Yes, they have sinned and deserve your judgment. But in my sacrificial death, I've already taken that judgment.*

☑ Apply

There are always plenty of people (including in churches) saying that our lifestyles don't matter too much; that we're not too bad; or that particular sins are excusable. John says, *They do; we are; and they're not.*

❓ *How do you find yourself making each of these three false claims?*
❓ *How do 1:7, 9, and 2:1-2 encourage you to accept that you're a sinner, confess your sins and seek to live a pure life?*

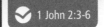
Do you know Jesus?

That's a question that some of us are worried about when we don't need to be; and perhaps others of us are complacent about it when we shouldn't be.

In the next section of the letter, John gives us three ways to be able to discern the truth about our relationship with Jesus. Today, we're looking at the first...

Read 1 John 2:3-6

The test

❓ *How do we know that we have come to know Jesus (v 3)?*

❓ *How is this challenging?*

This is no different from what Jesus himself taught: "You are my friends if you do what I command" (John 15:14). We should allow ourselves to be challenged by this if there are ways in which we are not doing what he commands.

But remember, these verses in John's letter come after 1 John 2:2, where John reminds us that if we do sin, Jesus Christ defends us in the heavenly court. So John is not insisting that only perfect people really know the perfect Christ. He's saying that only people who are committed to pursuing perfection truly know Christ. As the 16th-century Reformer John Calvin put it, John means "those who strive, according to the capacity of human infirmity, to form their life in obedience to Christ".

The liar

❓ *What kind of person is described as a "liar" (v 4)?*

TIME OUT

❓ *What might that type of person look like in your church today?*

❓ *Are there any ways in which you have ever been, or are today, at risk of being such a person?*

The result

❓ *What happens as we obey God's commands in his word (v 5)?*

❓ *How is this a motivation to obey God?*

So, here's the first test: "Whoever claims to live in him must live as Jesus did" (v 6), pursuing a life which is radically committed to obeying God, no matter what the cost or consequence. It's part of the letter's theme: *we know we know Christ if we seek to live like Christ—by obeying the Father* as he did.

☑ Apply

❓ *In what ways are you obeying God's commands well? How are you struggling? What will you change?*

⌃ Pray

Evaluate yourself using this first test of real Christian discipleship. Where you fall short, use 2:1-2 to confess and find forgiveness. Where you are battling hard, pray for courage and strength. Where you are obeying, thank God for his gracious work in you.

He reigns

Imagine the scene: trumpets blasting, huge crowds cheering, and a king leaping and dancing with very few clothes on…

That's the scene described when David and the Israelites brought the ark of the covenant back to Jerusalem after it had been captured by the Philistines as described in 1 Chronicles 16:2. No wonder these words pulsate with energy!

Above all gods
Read Psalm 96:1-9

❷ *What words are used to describe God in these verses? Which ones are repeated most often?*

❷ *What are people told to do in these verses? Find as many verbs as you can.*

❷ *When are we meant to do this (v 2)? Where (v 3)?*

Nothing can compare with this King (v 4-5)! So "proclaim[ing] his salvation" never gets old (v 2).

⌄ Apply

❷ *This week, how could you give God glory (that is, show how great he is)…*
- *with what you say with your mouth?*
- *with how you live your life?*
- *with what you do with your money (v 8)?*

God has always wanted "all peoples" to hear of his salvation. But in the New Testament, this emphasis becomes even clearer. **Read Matthew 28:18-20.**

❷ *Think of a non-Christian friend or co-worker. How would you explain Christ's "marvellous deeds" to them in a couple of sentences?*

The heavens rejoice
Read Psalm 96:10-13

These words look forward to the day of the Lord, when God will renew creation and "judge the peoples" in a way that is 100% fair (v 10, 13). The excited reaction of the natural world shows us that this will be a wonderful day for God's people (v 11-12)— and so we are to urge those around us to be ready for it too (v 10).

···· **TIME OUT** ·······································

Today, go on a walk or watch a nature documentary. Notice what is beautiful; then imagine the trees, fields and clouds singing for joy (v 11-13). All that is good in creation now is just a glimpse of what it will be like on the day when everyone sees that "the LORD reigns"—the day when he puts the whole world to rights. Every branch and stone will resound with delight.

⌃ Pray

Talk to God about your answers to the "Apply" questions. Ask him to help you to declare his glory to people you know.

All you need is…

The first test was about obedience to Christ. Here's the second, and it's no less challenging.

A crucial command

Read 1 John 2:7-8

John is talking about a command that is "old" (v 7) and "new" (v 8)! Here's my best guess as to what he means. It is a command which is absolutely foundational to the Christian faith—we have known it from the beginning of our Christian lives. Yet it is also a "new command", which must be lived out daily, in new and different ways, according to the circumstances each day brings.

> ❷ *What does John say about the darkness and the light (v 8)?*

In other words, we live in the dawn—in a time when the world is still sinful (dark), but Christ (light) has come to it, and it is heading for the perfect light of God's presence (Revelation 22:5). So the question is: *are we part of the coming day or the passing night?* The way we live out this old-new command will show which we belong to.

What is the command?

Read 1 John 2:9-11

> ❷ *What shows that someone is in the darkness, whatever they may say (v 9)?*
> ❷ *What shows that someone lives in the light (v 10)?*

So, what is the command? Jesus said, "My command is this: love each other as I have loved you" (John 15:12). The way we treat fellow Christians displays our true status before Christ. *We know we know Christ if we seek to live like Christ—by loving God's people as he did.*

 Apply

In Jesus' and John's vocabulary, we either love or hate. And if we love, we love like Christ. This means it's very easy to hate brothers and sisters in quiet, private, polite ways. We do it any time we don't want what's best for a brother or sister, won't fully forgive them, or aren't prepared to sacrifice our own comforts or interests for them.

> ❷ *Who do you know who loves like Christ?*
> ❷ *Who do you love like this?*
> ❷ *Who do you need to start loving like this?*

By this stage, John's readers (and we) could be forgiven for wondering if they're really Christians! So John describes the youngest readers ("children"), the eldest ("fathers") and those in between ("young men").

Read 1 John 2:12-14

> ❷ *How does he reassure them?*
> ❷ *In spiritual terms, would you describe yourself as a child, a young man or a father?*
> ❷ *How is the description of your spiritual stage here true of you?*

Christians shouldn't love

As Christians, we are to love fellow Christians. But the Christian life is not all about love…

Do not love…

Read 1 John 2:15

❷ *What must we not love?*
❷ *If we do love it, what does this show?*

"The world" refers to the world as it is now: a world living in rebellion against its Maker, which "did not recognise" Christ (John 1:10). Yet "God so loved the world that he gave his one and only Son" (John 3:16)—shouldn't we love it too?! Yes, and no. God loves sinners in the sense that he has borne a cost to save them from their sins; we find it very easy to love sinners in the sense that we want to share in their sins. John is saying, *Don't join in with the ways of the world.*

The ways of the world

Read 1 John 2:16

John describes what the world is like in three ways:

1. "The lust of the flesh"—our innermost natural desires always tend towards doing what is ungodly. We desire what is disobedient to God and bad for us.

2. "The lust of the eyes"—we see only at a superficial level, and we long for what is new, popular and shiny, without thinking about what lies underneath. This is the attitude that sees beauty but does not care for goodness or that sees popularity but does not care about integrity.

3. "The pride of life"—if we don't find our sense of worth in Christ, we seek it in our achievements or acquisitions—boasting about what we have and what we do. The world pursues nicer stuff, better careers or more good deeds, so that it can tell others and feel good.

TIME OUT

Think through each category and identify ways in which you're tempted to love the way the world works in each of them.

Remember…

Read 1 John 2:17

❷ *What must we remember, negatively and positively, in order to resist the world?*

TIME OUT

For each of the temptations to love the world's ways that you picked out earlier, think about how verse 17 can motivate you to love God, not the world.

▲ Pray

The best way to love the world less is to love the Lord more. You already have in Christ Jesus everything that the world is seeking: true satisfaction, security and worth. Pray that you would find those things increasingly in him, and so be enabled to resist pursuing them in worldly ways.

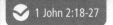
The third test

We know we have come to know Christ if we seek to obey as he did, and to love as he did. Here's the third test of true discipleship.

Antichrist(s)
Read 1 John 2:18-19

"The antichrist" probably refers to a man who "is coming", to proclaim himself to be Christ (see 2 Thessalonians 2:3-4, where he's called "the man of lawlessness"). In the meantime, "many antichrists have come" (1 John 2:18). These people oppose the truth about Jesus—they are anti Christ.

❷ *How have they identified themselves (v 19)?*

❮ Pray

Sometimes, it is right for Christians to leave a church which has ceased teaching the truth. At other times, it's right to stay and oppose error, waiting for "antichrists" to leave.

Pray now for anyone you know who is seeking to hold to the truth in their church but is being opposed by those who reject the teaching of the Bible.

Anointed
Read 1 John 2:20-25

❷ *If you have an "anointing" from the Holy Spirit, what do you know (v 20)?*
❷ *What is the lie that some people are promoting (v 22)?*

John is saying that anyone who denies that Jesus is the Christ (God's appointed, eternal King) and/or denies that Jesus Christ is the Son of the Father (the man who is divine) is "antichrist", a "liar". The worst lie anyone can believe or promote, however politely they may do it, is that Jesus is not the Christ and not the Son.

❷ *If the truth about Jesus—"what [we] have heard from the beginning"—remains what we believe, what happens (v 24-25)?*
❷ *So why is believing a lie about Jesus so horrendous?*

Astray?
Read 1 John 2:26-27

❷ *Why is John writing (v 26)?*

In verse 27, John promises that the Spirit—"the anointing"—teaches us the truth and protects us from error. That does not mean that we don't need teachers who remind us of the truth about him—after all, John is doing just that as he puts pen to paper!

❷ *How do we escape being led astray, according to the last three words of v 27?*

In other words, *we know that we know Christ if we hold to the truth about Christ.*

❮ Pray

Pray for yourself today, and for the day of your death. Pray that you would hold to the truth about Christ every day between now and then. Pray for anyone you know who seems to be going astray.

Back to obedience

Obedience… love… holding to the truth: the three tests of true faith. Next, John will return to each in more detail. Today and tomorrow, we're looking at obedience.

If we continue
Read 1 John 2:28-29

> ❷ *If we "continue in him", what can we look forward to when Jesus comes back to this world (v 28)?*
> ❷ *How do you feel about this prospect?*

What does it look like to "continue in him" moment by moment until the day when Christ comes? If we know the truth about him—"that he is righteous" (v 29)—then we'll seek to live like him—to do "what is right", both in our actions and our attitudes. We'll love our neighbour out of love for our God. If we know the character of our Lord, we'll seek to shape our character according to his—to remould ourselves to his pattern.

And this way of living shows that we are "born of him". Those three words are so mind-blowing that John pauses to enjoy them (3:1)…

Our identity
Read 1 John 3:1-2

> ❷ *What are believers in Christ called (v 1)?*

Just pause here. How great is this love?! The Creator, the Sustainer, the Ruler, the eternal, all-powerful God calls you his child. He identifies himself as your Father. He loves you as a parent. Wow! *Spend some time thanking your Father that you're his child.*

> ❷ *As children of God, what don't we yet know (v 2)?*
> ❷ *What do we know (v 2)?*

We are children of God, heading for our heavenly family home. You and I simply cannot imagine the glory that we are destined for when we get there. We cannot imagine it—but one day, we will see and experience it.

How it changes us
Read 1 John 3:3

> ❷ *What difference does knowing who we are and where we're heading make to us right now?*

If we know Christ's character, we'll seek to copy it (2:29)—we'll obey God as he did. If we know our identity, we'll seek to live pure lives—we'll want to live like our Brother, and for our Father.

☒ Apply

Think of a sin you find yourself committing over and over again.

Next time you're tempted in that way, say to yourself, "I know Jesus. I know I am a child of God. Am I really going to act as though I don't know him and don't have a heavenly Father?"

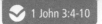

Why Jesus came

We obey as we look forward to the righteous Christ's future appearance, when we're welcomed home as God's children. Next, John looks back to Christ's first appearance.

All sin

Read 1 John 3:4-7

"The law" here refers to God's law—his moral standards for life in his world.

❓ *What does "everyone who sins" do (v 4)?*

We find it very easy subconsciously to put sins into categories: excusable or non-serious (these tend to be the sins we or our friends commit) and inexcusable or very serious. So a bit of gossip or a little drunkenness or a few jokes involving innuendo don't matter too much. Murder and sleeping around, on the other hand...

❓ *How does verse 4 challenge that?*

No sin is exempt; no excuse is valid.

❓ *How does this motivate us to obey God?*
❓ *Why did Jesus appear 2,000 years ago (v 5)?*

Here we see how serious sin—yours and mine—is. The Son of God had to come to earth as a man, and die on a cross, to take it away, so that we would not face the terror of judgment.

❓ *How does this motivate us to obey God?*
❓ *What does John say the result is if we live "in him" (v 6)?*

Remember, John is not saying a Christian "stops sinning" but that they do not "keep on sinning" without caring, without crying, without confessing.

✅ Apply

❓ *In which part of your life—thoughts, motives, words or deeds—do you need to apply these verses and this challenge?*

Behind the sin

Read 1 John 3:8-10

❓ *Who lies behind all sin (v 8a)?*
❓ *Why did Jesus appear 2,000 years ago (v 8b)?*

So, if we're "born of God", how can we go on living as though we're children of the devil? (If you have time, read through John 8:42-44.) How can we align ourselves with the work of the one who wants to destroy life—the one whom the Son of God came from heaven to destroy by dying on a cross?

❓ *Why is 1 John 3:10 an inevitable implication of verses 8-9?*

🔼 Pray

Identify and confess your sin. Work out how you can obey in those areas of your life instead, and ask God to help you. Meditate on what Christ did for you when he first appeared, and what Christ will do for you when he next appears, and let that motivate you to reject sin and live for him today.

Back to love

Now, John turns again to the second marker of the real Christian: "We should love one another" (1 John 3:11).

Hated by the world

Read 1 John 3:11-18

❓ *What did Cain do? Why (v 12)? (If you have time, read Genesis 4:2b-12.)*

In John's thinking, Cain represents the world: Abel, the faithful. Cain could not stand Abel being favoured above him. Since he couldn't compete with Abel, he killed him. That's the way of the world: dragging ourselves up—dragging others down; ultimately, what matters is me. So "do not be surprised, my brothers and sisters, if the world hates you" (1 John 3:13)—Cain hated Abel, and the world will feel threatened by a people who don't live like them and don't strive like them and yet enjoy the security and fulfilment that the world is chasing.

❓ *How did Jesus Christ show a different way to that of the world (v 16)?*

And he is not only our great Saviour; he is also our great example (v 16b).

❓ *What does this mean for us practically, day by day (v 17-18)?*

✔ Apply

❓ *How well do verses 17-18 describe you?*
❓ *How could you, this week, lay down just a part of your "life" in order to love a brother or sister in need? Will you do that?*

Hearts at rest

Read 1 John 3:19-24

Notice that this section is bracketed by the words "this is how we know" (v 19, 24). Verse 19 looks backwards—we know we belong to "the truth" if we are people who are so filled up with Christ's sacrificial love for us that it overflows in our treatment of other Christians.

❓ *When does this give us "rest" (v 19-20a)?*

Most of us worry from time to time that we may not be saved. At these moments, sometimes we're able to look at our own love for others and "set our hearts at rest", by seeing that we only live like this because we know Christ died for us. But at other times, our hearts condemn us rightly; and then we can look at Christ's love for us and "set our hearts at rest" by telling ourselves that he died for us to cleanse our hearts (1:9; 2:2).

❓ *What's the impact of having a heart "at rest" (v 21-22)?*

✔ Apply

Is your heart struggling to be at rest? Look at your life—is there evidence of Christian love, to give you confidence? If not, repent and look at Christ's life and death—there is the evidence that you are forgiven, so take confidence!

Darkness and light

Psalms 97 to 100 all focus on God's majesty. Like the one before it, Psalm 97 looks forward to God's coming as King on the day of judgment.

Darkness descends

Read Psalm 97:1-9

❷ *Given verse 1, in what sense do verses 2-5 come as a surprise?*

❷ *Why has the writer chosen to order the psalm in this way, do you think?*

These words are intended to remind us of when God gave the Ten Commandments to Moses. "Mount Sinai was covered with smoke, because the LORD descended on it in fire ... and the whole mountain trembled violently" (Exodus 19:18). God's coming in the future will be as real to our senses as it was that day for the Israelites. At Sinai, the Israelites were warned not to approach God because of his blistering holiness. But on the day of the Lord, God's blistering holiness will approach us...

❷ *What two different responses do we see to God's coming? (Compare verses 7 and 8 of Psalm 97.)*

☑ Apply

❷ *How have you heard people around you "boast[ing] in idols" this week? (And how have you done so yourself, perhaps?)*

❷ *When you hear this kind of boasting in others, how are you tempted to respond (on the inside at least)?*

❷ *How will these verses shape your reaction next time?*

Tune in to conversations in public places, and you'll hear people bragging about everything from sporting success to sexual conquests. And it is easy to be either quietly impressed or secretly jealous. So we need to remember that these things are passing away (v 7). Instead, we rejoice because of the Lord (v 8)—something the final three verses emphasise...

Light dawns

Read Psalm 97:10-12

❷ *What two things are we told to do in these verses? What reason does the psalmist give?*

❷ *What has God got that idols haven't?*

A better translation of verse 11 is "light dawns". Perhaps your circumstances seem very dark at present. Hold on: the dawn is coming. On the day of the Lord, if we're trusting in Christ, he will guard us—body and soul (v 10). And that means we can rejoice today too (v 12). Even when we feel unable to rejoice in our circumstances, we can "rejoice in the LORD". We can praise God for what he is like ("holy") and for what he has promised to do for us in the future.

▲ Pray

"Rejoice in the LORD." Make a list of some of God's characteristics and praise him for each one.

The test

Do you tend to be overly credulous or overly critical? To believe all you hear or doubt all you hear?

Don't...
Read 1 John 4:1

❷ *What mustn't John's "friends" do?*
❷ *What should they do instead? Why?*

How to distinguish
Read 1 John 4:2-3

❷ *How can we recognise those through whom the Spirit of God is speaking?*
❷ *How can we spot those through whom the "spirit of the antichrist" is speaking?*

Verse 2 sounds very simple—as though we check someone believes in Jesus Christ and then relax. But actually, John is setting a much more detailed test here. The question is: do you believe that...

• "Jesus..." (a name meaning "God saves"—that this person is the means by which God rescues us from our sins)

• "Christ..." (i.e. anointed one, God's chosen King—that this person is the means by which God rules his world)

• "has come..." (that he came from heaven—he existed before he took up human flesh)

• "in the flesh" (that he came to earth and lived as a man, as human as us, in history)?

Often, we can either credit church teachers too much or too little: to be too quick to listen to them because they are friendly, funny or fine-looking; or too quick to dismiss them because they aren't like us, don't grab

us or don't have a look that fits. John says, *There's only one test. Use it, and don't add to it.*

TIME OUT

❷ *How about your attitude to your church's leaders? Would applying John's test, and only John's test, cause you to respect them more or resist them more?*

You have overcome
Read 1 John 4:4-6

❷ *Whose viewpoint do the "antichrist" teachers represent (v 5)? Why will this make them popular, inside churches as well as outside?*
❷ *In what sense will fewer people listen to faithful Bible teachers than to antichrist church leaders (v 6)?*

In the midst of all this, verse 4 is very reassuring! Real Christians—"dear children"—will "overcome" false teachers because the one who dwells in us, works in us and looks out for us is far more powerful than the one who (though they may not realise it) is working through false teachers.

▲ Pray

Thank God for those who teach that Jesus Christ has come in the flesh, week in, week out. Pray for their ongoing faithfulness, even though it may lead to unpopularity.

Bible in a year: 1 Chronicles 28-29 • Luke 4:31-44

This is love

The next section contains some of the most well-loved verses in the whole of Scripture. We'll take two days to enjoy it.

Read 1 John 4:7-11

What God has done

❷ *What does John say about God in these verses?*

❷ *How has God shown his love (v 9-10)?*

"Atoning sacrifice" (v 10) is the same phrase John used back in 2:2. Through his sacrificial death, Christ bore all that stands between us and God—our sins and his judgment of them—so that we could be "at-one" with our Maker again.

^ Pray

This is the entry point to the Christian life. It is also the continuing foundation for the Christian life. Yet how easy it is to forget it, or take it for granted, or lose any sense of wonder that God did this.

Spend some time now using 4:9-10 to praise God for what he is like and what he has done for you.

What we must do

❷ *What does John tell his "dear friends"— Christians—to do (v 7, 11)?*

❷ *What motivations for doing this do those two verses give us?*

If you struggle to love fellow Christians in a wholehearted, sacrificial way, putting their best before your comfort or ease, the answer is not to try to love them more! It's not even to try to love God more! It is to reflect on God's love for you. We only find ourselves loving fellow Christians—no matter who they are, what they're asking for or what they've done to us—if we begin our thinking with "Since God so loved me..."

✓ Apply

❷ *What would change this week if, before you decided on how to fill your diary and use your bank balance, you said to yourself, "Since God so loved me..."?*

Seeing God

Read 1 John 4:12

❷ *What does this verse suggest about...*
- *how people can see God today?*
- *how we can fully experience and enjoy God's love?*

^ Pray

The people in our local communities have never seen God. But they do see our churches. Pray that your church would display such a different quality and commitment of love that God would be made visible, and would be shown to be wonderful, to those around you.

Because he loves you...

Day 2 in this wonderful passage... and John wants us to see three ways in which knowing God loves us makes a total difference to how we feel and live.

Difference 1

Read 1 John 4:13-16a

How do you know God loves you and lives in you? John offers subjective proof—you experience his presence in your life, through his Spirit (v 13). And then he offers objective truth—you know that Jesus is the Son of God (v 15), who came to save you (v 14).

> ❷ *And so we do what two things (v 16)?*

Christians do both. We don't just understand God's love—we live by it. Everything is shaped by it. We allow our decisions about how to live, where to live, who to live with and so on to be guided by the knowledge that God loves us. It is God's love—and no one else's and nothing else—that we look to for our security and joy.

Difference 2

Read 1 John 4:16b-19

> ❷ *If we know God is love, what do we have (v 17)?*
> ❷ *What don't we have (v 18)?*

We can only live like this if we know that "we love because he first loved us" (v 19). If we think our love earns God's love or keeps God's love, we will be fearful and have no confidence. When we fail to love well, we'll think, "Now God might not love me". When life goes wrong, we'll wonder, "Is God punishing me for something I've done?" But "he first loved us"—our love is a response to his, not a precursor to it. He loves us because he loves us—so he will love us today, and he will love us on our last day. There's no need to be afraid, ever!

Difference 3

Read 1 John 4:20-21

> ❷ *John mentions a sign of being loved by God. What is it (v 19-20)?*

This continues John's thought from verse 16: "Whoever lives in love lives in God, and God in him". John is saying that only if we know we're loved by God will we truly love others. How can this be? Because without knowing he loves us, all the good we do for others will have an aspect of self-love—we'll be doing it for their approval or to feel good about ourselves or to make God love us. But if we know he loves us—if we rely on it and are confident in it—we can love others without any thought for ourselves. God's love frees us to love others.

⌄ Apply

> ❷ *How are you relying on God's love today?*
> ❷ *How are you enjoying not being afraid today?*
> ❷ *How are you loving others because God loves you today?*

It's true

Remember our summary? We show we are in Christ if we live like him and hold to the truth about him. John now draws these together; then he focuses on the last part.

Us against the world

Read 1 John 5:1-5

❷ *How does verse 1 summarise what we've seen regarding holding to the truth about Christ?*

❷ *How does verse 3 summarise what we've seen about living like Christ?*

If we believe in Christ and seek to live like Christ, then we're in Christ, reborn as children of God (v 4a).

❷ *And what happens to everyone "born of God" (v 4)?*

"The world" is the realm of rejection of Christ, both in lifestyle and in teaching. "The world", as we've seen, can easily invade the church. But, while we cannot be complacent, we don't need to worry. If we know Christ, we'll seek to obey God as he did and love his people as he did and hold to the truth about him—and the world cannot touch us.

Three witnesses

Read 1 John 5:6-12

This is John's last extended exhortation on one of his themes—he focuses on the truth about Jesus (God saves) Christ (God's King).

There is some disagreement about what John means by "water" and "blood". But remember that he is countering false claims that if Jesus was truly "the Son of God"

(v 5), he was not truly human. So then, it's probable that he's thinking of Jesus' water baptism, where he identified with sinful humanity; and his bloody death, where he really died for sinful humanity. The Spirit testifies in us and to us that Jesus is the divine human; the water and the blood—the historical record—agree (v 8).

❷ *What do we do with this testimony (v 9-10)?*

John is making a stark point in v 10. God has said Jesus is his Son—his Spirit, the baptism of Jesus, and the death of Jesus all say the same thing about who he is. If we decide to believe Jesus is not God's Son or not fully human, we are saying that God is a liar. Unbelief, however politely expressed, is no small matter. It is calling God a liar.

TIME OUT

❷ *How might this help you to challenge someone who believes in God but not in his Son?*

❷ *What is wonderful about knowing the truth about Jesus (v 11-12)?*

⌃ Pray

Thank God for his testimony about who Jesus is. Thank him for the historical events of Jesus' life and for the work of the Spirit in you. Thank him that as you remain in Christ, you overcome the world.

Know you have life

John now reaches the end of his letter with a purpose statement, two promises, a summary and a final challenge.

Purpose

Read 1 John 5:13

❓ *Who is John writing to, and why?*

If we believe, we have eternal life. But we need, in the daily grind of life in this world, to *know* we have life. We need to remember that it's true and that it's wonderful.

Promises

Read 1 John 5:14-17

❓ *How can we believers be confident as we pray (v 14-15)?*
❓ *What else can believers do (v 16)?*

It's not quite clear what all of verses 16-17 mean! But the clearest part of them (relatively speaking) suggests that we can play a role in the way that God restores one of his children who has wandered away. When we see a brother or sister sin, we shouldn't excuse it or ignore it or think it's their issue. We should pray for them.

---- **TIME OUT** ....

It's not clear what "the sin that leads to death" is—but Jesus' death is sufficient to cover all sins (2:1-2), so it's likely that "the sin that leads to death" is the sin of refusing to ask Jesus to forgive us. Which, by definition, no Christian is committing; and so we will pray for that person very differently—for them as a non-Christian, not as a believer.

Summary and challenge

Read 1 John 5:18-20

John outlines his main message one last time. Anyone born of God...
- v 18—seeks to obey him, instead of sinning.
- v 19—is a child of God, and will love like him instead of being like the world, like Cain (3:11-13).
- 5:20—knows the truth "that the Son of God has come" to bring us "eternal life".

In other words, *we know we know Christ if we seek to live like Christ and hold to the truth about Christ.*

Read 1 John 5:21

One of the most dangerous idols to worship is a made-up Jesus. This Jesus—who does not call us to obey or to love sacrificially or to believe he is divine and the only way to have eternal life—is easier to follow and more popular in the world but cannot save.

⬇ Apply

❓ *How has the letter of 1 John...*
- *helped you enjoy God's love more?*
- *caused you to love him more?*
- *prompted you to obey him and to love his people in a new way?*
- *given you confidence that what you believe is true?*

Use your answers to fuel your prayers now.

GENESIS: Ordinary Joe?

Genesis 36 drew the curtain on Esau and his family. Attention now turns to Jacob's family, the line to whom God's covenant belongs, finally settled in the land of promise.

Happy families?
Read Genesis 37:1-11

❷ *How happy do you think Jacob's family was? Examine...*
- *the description in verse 2.*
- *Joseph's behaviour.*
- *Israel's (Jacob's) attitude (v 3).*
- *the reaction of Joseph's brothers (v 4).*

❷ *What has Jacob learned from his own family history (compare 25:28)?*

The problem of favouritism in a family can be very acute, especially when inheritance is involved. Half-siblings and step-siblings in particular can feel left out. So it is with Joseph's brothers, especially those born to Bilhah and Zilpah, the servants of Rachel and Leah (37:2).

Joseph fuels the fire with his bad report of them—well received by Jacob, who loved Joseph (first son of his beloved wife Rachel) more than his brothers (v 3). Worse, Jacob shows his favouritism by giving Joseph an immensely valuable robe. The brothers' hatred for Joseph, "daddy's boy" and snitch, is understandable—though not commend-able.

···· TIME OUT ····

Jacob, of all people, should have known the catastrophic damage that favouritism can cause.

Read Romans 2:11 and James 2:1, 9

❷ *In what areas do you need to imitate your heavenly Father?*

Arrogant
Re-read Genesis 37:1-11

Joseph is also arrogant and almost wilfully stupid, telling his brothers not just one but two dreams about his own greatness (v 5-9). Even Jacob finds the second dream too much (v 10)—the idea of parents bowing down to their son was completely unthinkable. But Jacob knew that dreams can be true (see 28:10-17). Despite his annoyance, Jacob reflects on it all (37:11)—rightly, since the plans of God hinge around Joseph.

☑ Apply

❷ *How would you have advised Joseph to behave?*
❷ *How could he have remained godly without being a total pain to his ungodly brothers?*

Moral uprightness needn't make us into prudes. Sometimes we need to be patient with people's moral failings.

Sing!

This psalm has strong similarities with Psalm 96—a remix, if you like, of a familiar tune. But this is a song we should never get tired of singing.

Sing it

Read Psalm 98:1-3

- ❓ *What reasons are we given for singing "a new song"?*
- ❓ *What word do we see repeated in all three verses?*
- ❓ *Who has seen all this (v 2-3)?*

In Revelation we get a glimpse of another "new song" sung by the company of heaven. **Read Revelation 5:9-10.**

- ❓ *In Psalm 98:1 God "worked salvation". How?*
- ❓ *What do you find most "marvellous" about it?*

Through Christ, God faithfully fulfilled the promises made to Israel (v 3). But it gets better: now people to "the ends of the earth" not only get to witness salvation but also experience it themselves. And it is all God's work: "He has done ... his right hand ... the LORD has made..." We need only see his salvation and receive it.

This is truly "marvellous". It is worth singing about!

Pray

Sing to God for his marvellous work of salvation. Pray for people, both those close to home and around the world, whom you long would see and receive it too.

Sing it louder!

Read Psalm 98:4-9

- ❓ *What different sounds are joining in the song? Close your eyes and try to imagine this euphony of praise!*
- ❓ *Why do they sing (v 9)?*

Verse 9 could be seen as a bit of a surprise. The creation sings for joy because God comes to "judge the world". But for believers, the day of judgment will be a day of salvation. "He comes" to make everything right and remove all our sorrow and sin.

And for the creation, that day will usher in a wonderful new era. The apostle Paul writes that "the creation waits in eager expectation for the children of God to be revealed" (Romans 8:19). On that day, the curse of sin will be removed. Rivers will no longer flood; they'll clap their hands. Mountains will no longer landslide; they'll sing for joy.

Apply

Every time we sing together as God's people (Psalm 98:4-6), it's like a mini rehearsal for the day "he comes".

- ❓ *How will remembering Psalm 98 change the way you sing next time you are gathered with your church family?*

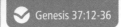

The brothers' revenge

Family disputes can be the worst. But this one goes way beyond squabbling at the dinner table and name calling. There is murder in the air...

Nightmare for Joseph
Read Genesis 37:12-24

- ❓ *How aware are Jacob and Joseph of Joseph's unpopularity?*
- ❓ *What drives the brothers to contemplate murder (end of v 20)?*
- ❓ *What might be behind Reuben's plan (see 35:22)?*

Joseph's worst nightmare begins in a matter-of-fact way, when his unsuspecting father sends him out alone to his brothers, an errand that he willingly accepts (37:13-14). By now their hatred has become truly murderous (v 18). Joseph is nicknamed the "dreamer" (v 19), but his brothers intend to show that his dreams are empty (v 20).

Reuben, already in disgrace (35:22), might see an opportunity to redeem himself by rescuing his father's favourite (37:22b); or perhaps, as the eldest, he knows he will be held responsible by his father. He persuades the brothers only to throw Joseph into an empty cistern, from which Reuben hopes later to rescue him. But this leaves for the others the problem of what to do with him, since he can hardly be allowed to go home and tell his father about the outrage.

Solution for the brothers
Read Genesis 37:25-36

- ❓ *What two things do the brothers gain from selling Joseph?*

There's no material gain in killing Joseph, and there would be real problems with hiding the body (v 26). But selling him provides both a profitable and a "moral" solution. Hands and consciences can both be clean (v 27), and pockets lined at the same time (v 28).

Reuben returns too late—despite his grief, he's now implicated and must go along with events (v 29-32). The brothers allow Jacob himself to invent the cover story—the sons merely have to agree with Jacob's conclusion that Joseph has been killed and eaten (v 33).

☑ Apply

This story, like our lives, is full of "what ifs?". So many people could have behaved better. Yet be encouraged that God's plan is unstoppable. He uses Joseph's arrogance, his brothers' hatred and Jacob's favouritism, but also allows his people to go through intense personal suffering.

- ❓ *What should we learn from this?*

A tale of two brothers

Later in the Bible, the book of Proverbs would give sound advice for Joseph's brothers generally, while Proverbs 6:20-26 would have been especially helpful to Judah...

Wilful neglect
Read Genesis 38

- ❷ *What can we conclude about Judah in view of his marriage (v 2, compare 24:3)?*
- ❷ *What's the reason for the deaths of Judah's two eldest sons (38:7, 10)?*
- ❷ *What does Judah appear to think the reason is (v 11)?*

By marrying a Canaanite Judah ignores his heritage, but God does not ignore his family. Judah's eldest son, Er, dies because of his wickedness (v 7). Then the second son, by seeking to deprive his widowed sister-in-law of heirs, also comes under judgment and dies (v 8-10). (God's command, implicit here, is later made explicit—see Deuteronomy 25:5-6.) Oblivious to the spiritual reasons for the death of his sons, Judah prefers to believe that his daughter-in-law is somehow "cursed".

Double standards

- ❷ *What is legitimate about the reason behind Tamar's dodgy plan?*
- ❷ *In what ways is Judah culpable?*

Judah himself provides an unwitting solution to his dilemma via Tamar's ingenuity. Knowing that Judah is holding out on her with regard to Shelah (Genesis 38:14b), Tamar deliberately entices Judah into thinking she is a prostitute (v 15-16a). The morality is dubious—even though her claim to progeny in Judah's line is legitimate. When her pregnancy becomes obvious (v 24), she saves her life by exposing Judah's shameless double standards. Judah is forced to acknowledge her (comparative) righteousness (v 26).

▲ Pray

Pray that you would be delivered from your own double standards.

Progeny

The younger of Tamar's twins will be the ancestor of David (see Ruth 4:18-22). Note again how God shows his delight in reversing the human social order!

In Matthew's genealogy of Jesus (Matthew 1) five women are mentioned—two prostitutes (including Tamar), a foreigner, an adulteress and a single mum. It's hardly the sort of pedigree that most people would want to publicise! Is this a slur on these women or, given that the single mum is Mary, might there be another lesson?

- ❷ *What is it?*

Back in Egypt

Good times had come to Joseph, elevated to high rank in an important household because of his obvious talents. But a mighty fall is waiting for him...

Meteoric rise

Read Genesis 39:1-6

- ❓ *As he didn't ignore Judah's family, so God doesn't ignore Joseph either. What's the outcome for Joseph?*
- ❓ *How is God's promise to Abraham of blessing to the world being fulfilled here (v 5-6)?*

In the years when Judah is experiencing his family problems, Joseph's fortunes almost irresistibly rise, not least because he acts with the kind of wisdom and integrity that Proverbs commends. God is with Joseph to bless him (v 2), just as he was with Judah to bring curses on his wicked family (38:7, 10). Moreover, through Joseph, Potiphar experiences a taste of the "world blessing" promised through Abraham (compare 39:5-6 with 12:3).

Sudden downfall

Read Genesis 39:7-23

- ❓ *How does Joseph's behaviour here compare with Judah's?*
- ❓ *As Joseph continues to act with honour and integrity, what's the outcome for him now?*

In his response to the attentions of Potiphar's wife, Joseph is exactly like the wise young man of Proverbs 5:1-14. To give in to the advances of Potiphar's wife would, in his view, be a sin against both God and Potiphar himself, who has trusted him with so much.

✅ Apply

It is sometimes suggested that Joseph was unwise to enter the house when Potiphar's wife was there (Genesis 39:11).

- ❓ *Does the text suggest Joseph was to blame (e.g. v 10)?*
- ❓ *What were Joseph's tactics when faced with repeated temptation?*

Pray for the same practical wisdom when you are faced with temptation.

Dreadful result

Although Joseph's behaviour continues to be exemplary, this time the outcome is an accusation of attempted rape (v 11-18) and unjust imprisonment by the outraged master he had tried to honour (v 20)—provoking the question: is God still with Joseph?

- ❓ *What's the answer (v 21, 23)?*

✅ Apply

We cannot assume that uprightness always results in good fortune, but we can be certain that the Lord is always "with" his people, and so it is always worth following Joseph's example, whatever the outcome may be.

More dreams

Joseph's gifting goes beyond his ability to run a household and a prison. He has spiritual gifts that make him unique.

Read Genesis 40:1-23

Servant

- ❷ *What's the status of the two new prisoners?*
- ❷ *What extra responsibility is Joseph given (v 4, compare 39:22-23)?*
- ❷ *How does Joseph carry out his new responsibilities (40:6-7)?*

Joseph must have suffered from stress, anxiety and boredom in prison. Then, when two new "guests" arrive—not menial servants, but honoured members of the court (compare Nehemiah 2:1-9)—Joseph has to serve them as well as run the prison (Genesis 40:4)! But an unexpected opportunity arises.

As in most cultures, the Egyptians recognised that dreams can be deeply significant, and so each official concludes that there must be a "message" involved in his vivid dream. But not knowing what it is, they are dejected when Joseph sees them the next day. Joseph's qualities, however, include sensitivity and compassion for those he serves (v 6). And when his enquiry about their mood discovers its cause, he can provide the answer, for he has had meaningful dreams of his own (see 37:5-11).

Prophet

- ❷ *Who is it that will interpret these dreams (40:8)?*
- ❷ *Joseph refuses the opportunity for self-promotion, but what opportunity does he seize at this point?*
- ❷ *How does his godliness appear to be rewarded?*

From the outset Joseph is at pains to point out that it is God, and not an interpreter, who really knows the meaning of dreams (40:8, see also 41:16). And so what follows is not an example of divination or psychology, but prophecy.

In the deliverance of the cupbearer, however, Joseph sees an opportunity for his own deliverance from unjust imprisonment (40:14-15). In the event, the cupbearer forgets about Joseph—the man who served him in prison—as soon as he is restored to his high post (v 23). But if Joseph had promoted himself as the interpreter of dreams—who knows?—he may have made a greater impression on the cupbearer and got out of jail earlier.

⌄ Apply

It can always be argued that ungodly behaviour pays greater dividends. That's what makes it so appealing.

- ❷ *How would you argue against that?*

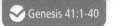
From prison to palace

A sudden reversal in fortunes can be very destabilising. Many people in rags do not take well to riches when they suddenly arrive. How will Joseph cope?

A long wait

Read Genesis 41:1-40

❓ *What does verse 1 reveal about what Joseph had to endure?*
❓ *What would you be thinking in his shoes?*

Joseph presumably believed God had a plan for his life, as should we. But what was he to do when for two years he couldn't discern the plan?

❓ *What does this true story reveal about...*
- *the world's most powerful man (v 8a)?*
- *the finest minds of the day (v 8b)?*
- *God's providential planning to get Joseph precisely where he wanted him to be (v 9-13)?*

Pharaoh is a man with extensive and absolute power but also a troubled mind. Once again the answer to the mystery lies not in the diviners (v 8), but with the Divinity (v 16). The prison incident—now a distant memory for Joseph and initially not even that for the cupbearer—proves to have been an essential part of God's plan, giving Joseph a spokesman in Pharaoh's court. The cupbearer's testimony quickly establishes Joseph's credentials (v 10-13) and he is duly sent for (v 14).

A rapid elevation

❓ *What is Pharaoh's verdict on Joseph (v 38-39)?*

The "discerning and wise man" (v 33) needed to implement Joseph's suggested 14-year national strategy is not hard to find, since even Pharaoh can see that the Spirit of God is in the man who stands in front of him (v 38-39). So Joseph is elevated from prison to a position second only to Pharaoh himself (v 40).

God used one man, filled with his wisdom, as the instrument of a great deliverance. Yet his plan was to save not just Egypt, Joseph, or even Joseph's family, but the world—when he would again use one man filled with his wisdom (see Matthew 12:42; 1 Corinthians 1:30).

⌃ Pray

When life seems to be going nowhere, despite our desire to do things for God, we needn't fret about being sidelined. Pray for patience in situations where nothing seems to be happening, and wisdom to seize the opportunity to serve God when it comes.

God's man in charge

Joseph's fortunes have changed dramatically, but they bring with them a whole lot of perplexing questions.

Fruitfulness

Read Genesis 41:41-57

- ❓ *What do you think is the reason for Joseph's new name and wife?*
- ❓ *How long has it taken Joseph to travel from slave to Pharaoh's second-in-command (v 46; 37:2)?*
- ❓ *Look at the Hebrew names Joseph gives to his sons (41:51-52). What does he forget and what does he remember?*

If Joseph is to be co-ruler over Egypt (v 44), he must become culturally Egyptian, hence the new name and Egyptian wife (v 45a). Only then can he begin his duties (v 45b).

Apply

Joseph's elevation from prison was no time to be picky. His change of name had to be accepted with good grace, although the gift of a pagan wife might have presented him with slightly more difficulties. But we should not compare our modern virtues and social norms with what happened back then.

- ❓ *Are there times when we should similarly swallow some of our principles? Is it always right to stick by them?*
- ❓ *When should we be flexible and when should we stand firm?*

Read 1 Corinthians 9:19-23 and think about your answers.

Joseph has used well the 13 years from his enslavement to this "moment of destiny" (compare Judah in Genesis 38). The prophetic dream of seven abundant years has come true, enabling Joseph to gather "grain mountains" so huge it isn't even worth keeping a tally of them (Genesis 41:47-49).

Joseph is personally fruitful as well, gaining two sons (v 50). They are given Hebrew names: "Forget"—perhaps in the sense of forgetting the past—and "Fruitful", reflecting the blessing Joseph has so remarkably received from God (v 52).

Apply

- ❓ *What do you need to forget (and forgive) today?*
- ❓ *What goodness from God do you need to remember (and thank him for)?*

Famine

Then the years of famine arrive "just as Joseph had said" (v 54, compare v 30-32)—these words reminding us again that, despite the widespread and desperate situation (v 57), God is firmly in charge.

Pray

Pray for confidence in God's sovereignty, both in your individual circumstances and when you look at the world scene.

Bible in a year: 2 Chronicles 28-29 • Luke 10:1-24

That God is your God

Have you ever read stories from the Old Testament and wished you could experience God's power like believers such as Moses, Aaron or Samuel did?

Fear

Read Psalm 99:1-5

❷ *Which of God's characteristics does the writer of this psalm emphasise?*

❷ *What is good about having God as King (v 4)?*

❷ *What problem does verse 4 present for sinful humans (that is, all of us)?*

Twice we are told that "he is holy" (v 3, 5). It's not just that God is wholly morally good (v 4)—he is also totally different and totally distinct from us. God's holy character alone is enough to make us kneel in awestruck worship (v 5). And yet there's more...

Forgiveness

Read Psalm 99:6-9

❷ *Can you think of specific times from the lives of Moses, Aaron and Samuel when these men spoke to God on behalf of the people? (Hint: Look up Exodus 32:9-14; Numbers 16:41-50; 1 Samuel 7.)*

❷ *What's the paradox, or problem, in Psalm 99:8?*

It's a paradox we see throughout the Old Testament: how can a holy King, who will punish sin because he is just (v 4), also forgive his people (v 8)?

And it's a paradox solved at the cross. **Read Romans 3:25-26.** In dying for us, Jesus became a priest greater even than Moses or Aaron—an intermediary between God and his people.

That means that every believer can have an intimate relationship with God like these heroes of faith from the Old Testament—or more intimate, in fact. God no longer speaks to us from a pillar of cloud at a particular time in a particular place; he lives in us by his powerful Spirit every day of our lives, and speaks to us through his word. And we can speak to him too. You can be "among those who [call] on his name" (Psalm 99:6)—and because you approach God on the basis of his Son's death for you, you can have even greater confidence than Samuel that the Lord will answer (v 6). In other words, you do experience the power of God, in a way that is, in a very real sense, actually greater than Moses, or Aaron, or Samuel did.

☑ Apply

"The Lord our God is holy"—and so we worship him (v 9).

❷ *How will you "exalt the Lord" (show that he's great, v 5, 9) in:*
  • *what you say to him now?*
  • *what you do this week?*

 Bible in a year: 2 Chronicles 30-31 • Luke 10:25-42

"Near-miss" reunion

While Egypt was well prepared for the famine, back in the land of Canaan, things are very different. And the strained dynamics of Jacob's family start to show...

Disaster looms
Read Genesis 42:1-20

> ❓ *What's the evidence here that the journey to Egypt was an act of desperation?*

The headstrong, wayward sons might have been good in a fight, but Jacob clearly feels that they are useless in a fix (v 1)! Although a trip to Egypt seems the obvious solution, the brothers are evidently reluctant to go, and Jacob, wary of further disaster, keeps back the remaining son of his beloved Rachel.

> ❓ *Why the pretence and harsh words from Joseph, do you think?*

Joseph's harsh words may result more from his own confusion than a desire to humiliate his brothers. Indeed, it's only when Joseph sees them bowing down before him that he remembers the dreams that caused his original problems (v 9a, compare 37:10).

But having started the masquerade, Joseph must keep it up. Thus the brothers are accused of spying (42:9b-12). When Joseph hears about Benjamin (v 13), he sets about "persuading" his brothers (v 14-17) to bring Jacob's youngest son—his own closest sibling—before this "God-fearing" Egyptian (v 18-20).

Disaster strikes
Read Genesis 42:21-38

> ❓ *What does the brothers' conversation show (v 21-23)?*
> ❓ *What reveals Joseph's good intentions?*

Joseph's tears reveal his true feelings towards his brothers. He seems genuinely moved by the signs of their slowly awakening consciences. Now he plans to test his brothers further. By returning their silver with the grain, he turns their fear into despondency and guilt (v 28) and then, ultimately, into panic (v 35)—will they keep the money and once again lie to their father?

They do neither, but when they arrive home, Jacob refuses to allow the deal to go through, even when Reuben offers two of his own sons as hostage for Benjamin (v 36-38). And so Joseph's longed-for reunion is postponed indefinitely.

⌃ Pray

Praise God for the gift of conscience. Though the pangs of a guilty conscience can cause us great suffering, the purpose of this gift is to bring us to God for confession, repentance, forgiveness and reconciliation.

Read Psalm 32 and pray through the thoughts it raises for you.

The return

Jacob faces a personal test as he struggles to balance powerful competing demands—hunger, love and fear.

Hesitation and delay
Read Genesis 43:1-15

Jacob is torn between wanting to protect Benjamin by keeping him at home and the urgent need to get more food from Egypt, which means sending Benjamin there to fulfil Joseph's demand (v 5).

> ❷ How does Jacob's anxiety show itself in verse 6?
> ❷ What's his main strategy for ensuring Benjamin's safe return (v 11-12)?
> ❷ Look at Jacob's opening words in verse 11 and his closing words in verse 14. What's his state of mind?
> ❷ How much faith in God's sovereignty does he truly have, do you think (v 14)?

Jacob is facing his worst nightmare—the loss of the only surviving son (as he sees it) of his beloved wife Rachel. He responds to the stress by lashing out petulantly and unjustifiably at his other sons (v 6), by setting things up as favourably as possible for the family delegation in Egypt, and finally, by descending into fatalism—"If I am bereaved, I am bereaved". In the midst of all this, his words about God in verse 14 sound more like a desperate last resort than a confident assurance of God's sovereignty.

☑ Apply

> ❷ Do Jacob's reactions to his stressful situation sound familiar?

> ❷ How do other parts of Scripture show a better way to respond (see Philippians 4:4-7, for example)?

Welcome and feasting
Read Genesis 43:16-34

Ironically, Jacob's sons now fear the very thing they inflicted on Joseph—enslavement (v 18). Their story about the silver is not completely truthful but Genesis faithfully records it, "warts and all". The steward is "in", not only on the truth, but on the underlying spiritual realities. "Your God," he assures them, has been at work (v 23a). And Joseph is both deeply moved at this reunion (v 30) and clearly enjoying himself (v 33-34).

☑ Pray

There are so many "what ifs" with this story. What if Joseph hadn't been so prudish, his father so divisive, his brothers so jealous? Certainly, many complications would have been avoided had everyone done what was right. Yet God's sovereignty overrules entirely.

Praise God—this is true for you, your family, your church and the gospel as well.

Insight

The tension begins to mount as Joseph tests his brothers. Will they pass, or will they fail?

Character test

Read Genesis 44:1-34

> ❷ *Why do you think Joseph doesn't reveal himself to his brothers during the feast?*
> ❷ *What is he hoping to reveal by insisting that Benjamin stays in Egypt as his slave (v 17)?*

Joseph wisely realises that his brothers have not yet been revealed to themselves (compare 42:21-24a). So he sets them a true test of character—*will they sacrifice another brother to save themselves?* Joseph's special cup is hidden in Benjamin's sack and, shortly after they leave, the steward is sent in pursuit. The words given to the steward (44:5) heighten the sense of divine retribution and also continue to mask Joseph's Hebrew identity (compare v 15).

Guilt revelation

Although the brothers are absolutely sure of their innocence (v 7-9), the discovery of the cup uncovers a deeper issue—they know they are guilty of a much greater crime (v 16) and so they admit they collectively deserve punishment.

> ❷ *What is significant about Judah's leadership here? (Compare 37:26-27.)*

Judah again rises to the occasion (see also 43:8-10). He points out the devastating impact on Jacob if Benjamin fails to come home (44:27-31) and offers himself as a substitute to spare his father's misery (v 33). It was Judah of course who came up with the plot to sell Joseph into slavery (37:26-27) and caused his father's misery over the first loss of a son. The subsequent guilt might also explain why Judah left home for a prolonged period (chapter 38). But now he is determined to spare his father any more misery, even at the cost of his own future (44:33). And thus the full impact of the last 20 or more years is revealed.

⌃ Pray

Guilt corrodes our lives and relationships.

A frank confession is what's needed. Think carefully before you speak to someone because sometimes confession can simply open old wounds, not heal them. But you must certainly bring the matter to the Lord.

Talk to God now about those things which still make you feel guilty.

And then **read 1 John 1:7** and rejoice.

Happy ending

The tense story reaches a stunning conclusion in a scene filled with emotions: love, anxiety, longing and fear. But at its heart is a powerful faith in God's goodness.

Revelation

Read Genesis 45:1-28

❷ *Why does Joseph's composure fall apart at this point (v 1-2; compare 44:33-34)?*

❷ *How does Joseph reassure his terrified brothers that they will not be harmed?*

❷ *How is Joseph's understanding of all that has happened to him linked to the promises God made to Abraham (45:7)?*

Joseph can no longer hide his feelings or his true identity, most likely because of the poignant reminder of his father's grief, or perhaps the remarkable sight of Judah's transformation from the jealous, vengeful schemer who enslaved his brother into the responsible and courageous protector of his family.

By contrast, the brothers are terrified as the young man they sold as a slave now has the power to destroy them all. But Joseph reassures them that there's no need for distress or self-recrimination (v 5a). All this time God has been at work to save the lives of this family to whom so much has been promised (v 5b-8), so why would Joseph now set about destroying them?

⌃ Pray

"In all things God works for the good of those who love him" (Romans 8:28). Easy to say, but often hard to see, except on rare occasions like this.

Pray for patience when you cannot see how things could possibly work out "for the good".

Reunion

❷ *How does God continue to open up the way for Joseph's family to be rescued from famine (Genesis 45:16-20)?*

Joseph plans that Jacob and the entire family will live in Egypt—in Goshen—not only to be near Joseph but also to survive the famine, most of which is still to come (v 10-11). And Pharaoh not only permits this but goes out of his way to welcome and provide abundantly for Joseph's family (v 16-23). Jacob's initial scepticism shows how demoralised he has become, but what he sees convinces him and his spirit revives (v 26-28).

☑ Apply

Review the path and progress of your life so far, thinking particularly of the way God has blessed you, even through the difficult times.

❷ *If God's amazing grace has brought you safe this far, will you trust that his grace will bring you home?*

Jacob's move

So far "the account of Jacob" (37:2) seems to have been about Joseph, his son. But now the focus shifts firmly back to Jacob (or Israel) himself.

Reassurance
Read Genesis 46:1-7

> ❓ *Why does God need to tell Jacob not to be afraid to go to Egypt (v 2-3)? (Genesis 15:12-16 might help.)*

Jacob is leaving the land promised to Abraham. Since God's words in Genesis 15:13 must have been known to Jacob, he would also have known that this move would bring oppression to his descendants. Doubtless this is why God reassures him in a vision (46:2-4)—one day the land will be re-entered, even though Jacob himself will be long-since dead.

⌄ Apply

The more Jacob understands of God's big plan for his people and how things will ultimately turn out, the more he can trust God, as Joseph did, through dark times.

Perhaps we find it hard to trust God when things get difficult because we understand poorly or we don't remind ourselves of God's big plan for his people. Read and reflect on **Ephesians 3:7-13.**

Roll call
Read Genesis 46:8-30

> ❓ *Why do you think the direct descendants of Jacob are listed like this at the point when the family is moving to Egypt?*

> ❓ *What's the connection with God's promises to Abraham?*

The "thirty-three" offspring of Jacob (v 15) seem in fact to be only 32 (Er and Onan being dead, v 12), but probably include Jacob himself (see bracketed note, v 8). However, the important point is that in the fourth generation from Abraham, God's chosen family are finally becoming numerous. God's promise of innumerable descendants of Abraham (15:4-5)—as well as his prediction about relocation to Egypt (15:13-16)—is being fulfilled.

⌃ Pray

Salvation has come to Abraham's family but in time this salvation will become a prison from which they will need saving again.

Praise God for our eternal salvation through Jesus Christ.

Settling down

As one who knows Egyptian ways, Joseph naturally handles the negotiations with Pharaoh as to where his family will live.

Separation

Read Genesis 46:31 – 47:6

- ❓ *Why does Joseph insist on an occupation for his family that the Egyptians find detestable (46:34)?*
- ❓ *How is Joseph's plan for his family in Egypt shaped by God's promise to Abraham (15:13-16)?*

Joseph's purpose is not just to secure the best land for them (47:6), but also to keep his family separate from the Egyptians (46:34b), so that they will not be assimilated into Egyptian ways. Joseph is thinking ahead to the time when God will call his descendants to return to the land of Canaan. They will be reluctant to go if they have come to feel "at home" in Egypt.

☑ Apply

Christians similarly look forward to a day when God will call us into his heavenly "promised land".

- ❓ *Does that prospect thrill you? Or do you feel too much "at home" in this world?*
- ❓ *Will you be distinctive as one of God's people, even if that makes you "detestable" to unbelievers?*
- ❓ *What action do you need to take to avoid being assimilated into this world?*

Blessing

Read Genesis 47:7-12

- ❓ *What's remarkable about this scene?*
- ❓ *Why does Pharaoh show Jacob such respect?*
- ❓ *How is God's promise about a blessing to all nations yet again being fulfilled?*

Here before the absolute ruler of a great world power stands Jacob—malnourished, unshaven, strangely dressed. Yet Jacob's age and experience are clearly striking (v 8) and give him the right to reverse the normal protocols (compare Hebrews 7:7).

Long life hasn't brought great happiness for Jacob. Yet as the inheritor of God's promise of world blessing—together with Abraham and Isaac—it's Jacob who blesses Pharaoh.

☑ Pray

We must never expect an easy ride, just because we serve the Almighty God.

Pray that your own difficulties may build up your faith so that you too may "bless" others.

Reasons to praise

The Reformer William Kethe wrote the hymn "All people that on earth do dwell" while in exile. This psalm, which inspired it, reveals why he was able to keep rejoicing.

Read Psalm 100

- ❓ *Who should be giving praise to God (v 1)?*
- ❓ *What reasons are we given for being thankful?*
- ❓ *When was the last time you "[shouted] for joy to the Lord"? What stops you from giving grateful praise:*
  - *in public (at church etc.)?*
  - *in private?*

Authentic worship is not fuelled by drums and smoke machines, but by the knowledge of God (v 3): namely, who God is (the Lord); who we are (creatures); and how we can relate to him (as his people).

And that's a very good thing, because even when we're not shouting for joy or worshipping with gladness, verse 3 is still true. We might be tempted to shout at God with frustration, or we find ourselves worshipping him without conviction, but we are still God's sheep. His love endures, even when your praise is lacking. He has already loved you for an eternity, and will love you for an eternity to come (v 5).

⌄ Apply

The first word of verse 2 is "worship" in the NIV, but "serve" in the ESV. These two ideas are inseparable.

Read Romans 12:1

- ❓ *What is true worship, according to this verse?*
- ❓ *What motivates true worship?*
- ❓ *What will it look like for you to be "a living sacrifice"...*
  - *over the next 24 hours?*
  - *over the next 7 days?*
  - *over the next 10 years?*

⌃ Pray

You've heard the psalm-writer's praise— now it's your turn to give grateful praise to God. Take your cue from the psalmist and frame your prayers of thanks around Psalm 100:5, informed by the knowledge of all that God has done for you.

- ❓ *In what ways have you experienced God's goodness? Read Acts 14:17. "Give thanks to him and praise his name"!*
- ❓ *In what ways has God shown his love for you? Read Romans 5:8. "Give thanks to him and praise his name"!*
- ❓ *In what ways has God proved himself faithful to you? Read 2 Corinthians 1:20. "Give thanks to him and praise his name"!*

Prosperity and posterity

In God's providence, Joseph's handling of the famine brings Pharaoh unimagined prosperity.

Prosperity

Read Genesis 47:13-31

❓ *What does Joseph take from the Egyptians in return for the gift of life?*
- *v 14:*
- *v 16:*
- *v 20-21:*

❓ *Do you think Joseph was unduly harsh in his treatment of the Egyptians?*

He takes the Egyptians' money (v 14-15), livestock (v 16-17) and finally their land and liberty (v 18-21)! Only the priesthood escapes with their land because Pharaoh already supplies them with food (v 22). The social structures of Egypt are permanently changed (v 26). Joseph also introduces a 20% tax on produce. It seems a very raw deal, but as the people themselves recognise, Joseph has saved their lives.

The others who prosper are the family of Israel (v 27). Unlike the Egyptians, they actually acquire property in this period—doubtless due to Joseph's protection.

☑ Apply

The Bible has a clear message for the superpower nations of this world. Read the words of God to another, later ruler of a world superpower.

Read Isaiah 45:1-7, 16-17, 22-25

❓ *What do we learn about...*
- *God's power over superpowers (v 1-3)?*
- *God's purposes in them (v 4, 5-7)?*
- *God's attitude to them (v 16, 24)?*
- *God's attitude to his people (v 17, 25)?*
- *God's desire for the nations (v 22)?*

Read Isaiah 60:1-12

❓ *What will the nations do for God's people?*
❓ *What will God's people do for the nations (v 2-3)?*

In Joseph's day, these truths were already being worked out in the relationship between Egypt and the family of Israel.

❓ *What lessons are there for us?*

Posterity

Re-read Genesis 47:28-31

❓ *What must Joseph do to show his father "kindness and faithfulness"?*

Despite his prosperity in Egypt, Jacob knows that the future lies in the land of the promise, hence his urgent wish to be buried there.

⌃ Pray

What dominates your thinking? Immediate prosperity or future blessing? **Read 1 Peter 1:3-5**—repent if needed and give thanks.

Right reversal

The God of the Bible is always counter-cultural and unexpected. As Joseph approaches his father to receive a blessing, we see this in the simple act of crossing hands.

New generation

Read Genesis 48

- ❓ *What status does Jacob confer on Joseph's two eldest sons (v 5)?*
- ❓ *Why, do you think (see v 11, 7)?*
- ❓ *What family pattern is repeated in verses 12-19 (compare 25:23 and 17:18-21)?*

Joseph knows Jacob's end is near (48:1), and also that there is unfinished business. Manasseh and Ephraim have a special place in Jacob's affections (v 11), and they will have a special place in God's plans, so Joseph brings them with him. After reminding Joseph of the covenant promise (v 3-4), Jacob declares that these two particular grandsons are to be treated as his own sons (v 5-6). Verse 7 suggests he also sees them as children of Rachel, who died prematurely in childbirth.

Joseph arranges the boys so that his father's right hand will naturally find the older (v 13), but, to his annoyance (v 17), his father crosses his arms to bless them (v 14), thus reversing the privilege of the firstborn. But though this might seem to be the result of failing eyesight or the confusion of old age, it is actually deliberate (v 19). Remembering Jacob's own background (25:23), however, this shouldn't surprise us.

---- **TIME OUT** ------------------

Read 1 Chronicles 5:1-2

Jacob's blessing reverses the rights of the firstborn twice. Joseph is given this status over Reuben, and Ephraim over Manasseh.

- ❓ *Why does God keep reversing the right of the firstborn?*

You can find answers in **Romans 9:10-16**.

Same promises

The phrase "he blessed Joseph" (Genesis 48:15) encompasses Joseph's two sons as well. They are blessed as themselves sons of Abraham, Isaac and Jacob (v 16b), and inheritors of the blessing of fruitfulness (v 16c). As for Joseph, God will be with him (v 21; compare 26:3), and will take him and his people ("you" and "your" are plural here) back to the land of promise (compare 15:16).

⌃ Pray

Praise God that his mercy and compassion do not depend on man's desire or effort.

The verdict: part 1

Jacob's sons assemble to listen to their father's final words…

Read Genesis 49:1-15

❓ *How appropriate is it to describe Jacob's words to his sons as "blessings"?*

❓ *What is really going on here (see v 28)?*

❓ *Which blessing stands out? Why?*

Reuben

❓ *How had Reuben at first excelled (v 3)?*

❓ *Why would Reuben "no longer excel" (v 4; compare 35:22)?*

As firstborn, the rights of seniority and leadership were his. But Reuben's character and morals failed him utterly. So he would "no longer excel" as the firstborn should.

Simeon and Levi

❓ *What was their failing? (See 34:25-29.)*

❓ *In what ways did Jacob's "blessing" fit their crime (49:6a, 7b)?*

Simeon and Levi's massacre in revenge for Dinah's rape was a disproportionate act of violent rage, not justice. So the inseparable avengers were to be ostracised (v 6a) and separated from each other (v 7b).

Judah

❓ *How has Judah shown leadership to his brothers (see 43:8-10; 44:18-34)?*

❓ *How does Jacob's blessing for Judah change in 49:10?*

Judah's blessing (v 8-9) is initially addressed to him personally. Judah (sounds like "praise") will be praised by his brothers as the conqueror of the family's enemies. But there is much more to this blessing than the others: a coming Ruler to whom the nations truly belong (v 10b) will bring an appropriate climax to Judah's rule (compare Ezekiel 21:25-27).

Zebulun and Issachar

Even the quiet, unremarkable one and the tough but lazy one get a mention.

These strangely named "blessings" are, in fact, verdicts "appropriate" (Genesis 49:28) to each son.

🔼 Pray

This "mixed bunch" were the foundational members of God's people (see Revelation 21:12). God's family now is also made up of gifted yet flawed people, whom he nonetheless uses for his own purposes and glory.

Praise God that he can use you through, and in spite of, your flaws and failings.

Praise God for your church, filled with flawed and damaged individuals. Pray that you would, together, be a remarkable testimony to the grace of God, and a signpost to his purposes in the world.

The verdict: part 2

The verdict of Jacob on his sons continues…

Read Genesis 49:16-28

❓ *Which of these verdicts stands out, and why?*

Dan

❓ *What was good and what was bad about Dan (v 16-17)?*

The vindicator of Rachel (30:6), Dan had the potential to be his people's judge (49:16), but was also capable of causing unexpected disaster (v 17; compare Judges 18). No wonder Jacob slips in a prayer for "salvation" (Genesis 49:18—"deliverance" in NIV: the word that gives us the name Joshua and Jesus).

Gad

As a border tribe, Gad (v 19) would often be raided but not easily overcome.

Asher

The "fat cat" of the family, Asher (v 20) would not only provide luxuries for Israel but would also enjoy them. But this life of luxury would sap the will to fight (see Judges 5:17).

Naphtali

Destined to be a tribe of beautiful character, Naphtali (Genesis 49:21) rose to the occasion under the leadership of Barak (see Judges 4:6-10).

Joseph

❓ *What's the reason for Joseph's steadfastness of character in hostile circumstances (Genesis 49:22-26)?*

Unsurprisingly, Joseph gets a big mention, but Jacob's words here focus just as much on "the Mighty One of Jacob" (v 24b), the one behind Joseph's character and good fortune—the "Shepherd" and "Rock" and God of his fathers, who had blessed him abundantly (v 25).

···· **TIME OUT** ···

❓ *How does Jacob's description of Joseph—"the prince among his brothers" (v 26)—anticipate Christ himself?*

Benjamin

Jacob's description of his youngest (possibly spoilt) son (v 27) as "a ravenous wolf" was proved true by the events of Judges 19 – 21, though Moses would have a kinder verdict (Deuteronomy 33:12).

🔼 Pray

In a "report" on your life, what phrase might God use to best sum you up? Too easily influenced by friends? Much unfulfilled potential? Too prone to fighting? Too interested in money? Lazy toad? Great worker?

❓ *What will you do about it?*

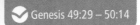
The death of Jacob

Inevitably, what first began with Adam back in Genesis 5:5, and has recurred in every generation since, is about to take place yet again…

Death

Read Genesis 49:29-33

> ❷ *What lies behind Jacob's final request (v 29-32)?*
> ❷ *How is his death described (v 33)?*
> ❷ *What does this tell us?*

As deaths go, this is a good one. Jacob is ready to depart this life. He knows where he wants his final resting place to be—in the cave purchased by Abraham from the Hittites (the only part of the land of promise that Abraham ever owned), where the other patriarchs and their wives are buried. This is not just the expression of an exile's longing for his fondly-remembered homeland, but the outworking of Jacob's continued faith in God's promises to his ancestors. Having thus given his final instructions, Jacob lies back and dies.

Jacob is "gathered to his people"—it's not just a euphemism for death, but also reflects the tremendous truth about death for God's people—see Hebrews 11:8-10, 13-16.

Grief

Read Genesis 50:1-14

> ❷ *What is Joseph's response, as a man of faith, to the death of his father?*

Despite it being a "good death" Joseph is distraught (v 1). Death is still an "enemy", and grief is appropriate (see John 11:32-35).

Burial

> ❷ *What shows the high regard in which Jacob, as father of Joseph, was held?*
> • Genesis 49:3:
> • v 6:
> • v 7-9:

Jacob's burial with "full honours" includes embalming by Joseph's own physicians (v 2-3a), an official period of mourning equivalent to a state funeral (v 3b), Pharaoh's personal permission for Joseph to leave Egypt (v 4-6), a huge escort to Canaan (v 7-9) and a lavish funeral ceremony that makes a lasting impression on the locals (v 10-11).

···· TIME OUT ·······································

Read 1 Thessalonians 4:13

> ❷ *What's the right balance between grief and hope?*

Pray for those who mourn, especially over the death of a parent.

✔ Apply

It might seem morbid to think about, or even plan your own funeral, but there is good reason for it.

> ❷ *How might your funeral give glory to God and expression to the gospel?*

And finally…

The book of Genesis concludes with a story of fear, grace and hope, as the eyes of God's people are fixed on the future when God's promises will be fulfilled.

Read Genesis 50:15-26

❓ *What thinking leads Joseph's brothers to send these (probably invented) instructions from their father?*

❓ *What thinking leads Joseph to treat them with grace?*

Guilt

Joseph's brothers remain in thrall to their guilt. With Jacob dead, the terrible thought occurs that Joseph might have waited for this moment to take his revenge (v 15). Perhaps this is how they would act in Joseph's shoes. Certainly, blood-letting among siblings after the death of their father is far from unknown. The fact is, Joseph's grace is incomprehensible to his brothers, because grace is incomprehensible to human nature generally.

Grace

So what makes Joseph so different? It's his unswerving trust in God's sovereignty (v 19-20). Joseph is free of vengeance because he leaves all matters of justice and punishment to the supreme Judge of all (v 19). Even if his own feelings were otherwise, how could he act as if he were God (v 19)? Joseph is also free of bitterness because he accepts that God allowed his suffering for a greater good—the saving of many lives (v 20).

⌃ Pray

❓ *Is your life still shaped by guilt, like the brothers?*

❓ *Or by grace through faith in God's sovereignty, like Joseph?*

Take time to talk to God about these things.

···· TIME OUT ····

"You intended to harm me, but God intended it for good to accomplish what is now being done, the saving of many lives."

❓ *How does Joseph foreshadow Christ (see Acts 2:22-24, 36; 4:27-28)?*

Faith

Characteristically, Joseph's last act is one of faith. Certain that God will one day bring his people out of Egypt to the land of the promise, Joseph makes his "brothers" (i.e. relatives) promise that his bones will be taken with God's people on the great journey (see Exodus 13:19; Hebrews 11:22).

⌄ Apply

"This world is not my home," says an old American song, "I'm just a-passing through".

❓ *Looking at how you live, would people guess this to be true for you, by the way you spend your time, money and leisure?*

King of kings

"A man is known by the company he keeps", or so the saying goes. And a person is formed, and shaped, by the leader he knows—as this psalm shows us.

This psalm was written by David as a summary of the kind of ruler he aspired to be.

King David

Read Psalm 101

- ❓ *What is David's personal standard for his own life (v 1-4)?*
- ❓ *What is his standard for those who serve him (v 5-7)?*
- ❓ *Did David meet his own standard? (Hint: Compare v 2 with 2 Samuel 11.)*

☑ Apply

This psalm is a portrait of the kind of rulers we all long to live and work under.

- ❓ *Can you think of a time when someone in authority over you failed to "conduct [their] affairs ... with a blameless heart"? How did you respond?*
- ❓ *Consider any positions of authority you hold. Do you share David's resolve to lead blamelessly?*

☝ Pray

Use this psalm to pray for the rulers of your nation. Pray that they would walk with personal integrity, choose their advisors wisely and value truth highly.

King Jesus

This psalm also points forward to the reign of King Jesus. **Re-read Psalm 101**, imagining these as the words of Jesus.

- ❓ *Do you meet the standard for serving as part of his household?*

- ❓ *When was the last time you...*
  - *dragged someone's reputation down (v 5a)?*
  - *looked down on someone (v 5b)?*
  - *twisted the truth in any way (v 7)?*

In the Gospels, Jesus embodies moral perfection. Yet, at the same time, he let a prostitute "minister" to him by washing his feet and he let fraudulent tax collectors eat at his table. Only Jesus is the blameless King of integrity that we long for. He perfectly encompasses both "love and justice" (v 1). He's the King who judges: every evildoer will be cut out of his eternal kingdom, along with all the hurt they cause (v 8). Yet he's also the King who loves: by his death on the cross he has made a way for wrongdoers to come into God's presence (v 7), and serve in his kingdom (v 6). There's no greater reason to "sing [his] praise" (v 1).

☝ Pray

Thank God that he's made a way for you to be part of his household—both now and in eternity. Pray that your life would look more and more like that of your King's.

CHRISTMAS: His names

Today, as we prepare for Christmas, we're starting a short series on the names that the Bible gives to the Lord Jesus, from Isaiah's famous prophecy.

❷ *Think about the different names that are attached to the Lord in Scripture. How many can you list?*

❷ *Which of them do you find the most powerful and attractive?*

❷ *Which of them do you find challenging or unsettling?*

Read Isaiah 9:6

In a famous passage, the prophet Isaiah promises that God will send a child who would be called "Wonderful Counsellor, Mighty God, Everlasting Father, Prince of Peace".

Isaiah is talking about the birth of Jesus that we celebrate at Christmas. He tells us some of the names by which Jesus will be known. In the Bible, names carry much more weight than they generally do today...

Name = authority

Imagine someone knocked on your door at 2am and said, "Open up in the name of Malcolm". You wouldn't be too impressed! But what if they said, "Open up in the name of the King"? You would scurry downstairs in your dressing gown to let them in. Names convey authority.

Read John 16:22-28

Jesus is talking about the time after his death and resurrection. Up till now he has prayed to the Father on behalf of the disciples. But after his death and resurrection his followers will be able to pray to God "in my name". God answers our prayers because we pray "in the name of Jesus". Sinful people can only come before God because they are cleansed by Jesus' blood. We have access to God through the death of Jesus on our behalf. As a result, we can pray as representatives of Jesus with the authority of Jesus.

And God will give us what we ask when we pray as the representatives of Jesus, praying for what Jesus would pray.

❷ *How did Jesus pray, and what did he pray for (scan John 17 if you need help)?*

❷ *How does that compare with the content and manner of your prayers?*

Name = character

In the Bible, names often also tell us something about a person's character. Jesus has many names to convey the richness of who he is and what he's done. That's why the name of Jesus soothes our sorrows and drives away our fear. Tomorrow we will begin looking at the names by which Isaiah says Jesus will be known.

Pray

What names for Jesus did you think about at the beginning? Talk to him now, using that name to shape your prayers for today— for the situations you face, and the people you know.

Revolution

"For to us a child is born, to us a son is given …
He will reign on David's throne and over his kingdom…" (Isaiah 9:6-7)

The son of David

Isaiah calls Jesus "a child … a son". It conjures up the cosy images of a thousand Christmas cards. But for Isaiah the gift of a son meant revolution.

For this is no ordinary son. He is the promised son of David. "He will reign on David's throne and over his kingdom." Isaiah is looking ahead to a time when God's people would go into the darkness of exile under the rule of foreign kings (see Isaiah 9:1-2). So the gift of a son meant revolution because it meant a king like David who would overthrow God's enemies and restore God's kingdom.

Read Luke 1:26-33

> ❓ *What new titles are given to Jesus by the angel Gabriel?*
> ❓ *How do they expand on the titles given by Isaiah?*

Read Luke 1:67-79

A "horn" (v 69) is a symbol of strength.

> ❓ *What new insight does Zechariah reveal about the revolutionary king to come?*

Zechariah sings of a mighty king from the house of David who will redeem his people from their slavery (v 68); save and rescue his people from their enemies (v 71, 74); so that they can serve God without fear (v 74-75).

Zechariah clearly has Isaiah's prophecy in mind (see v 70, 79 and Isaiah 9:2). He recognises that it is being fulfilled in the birth of Jesus and in the birth of Zechariah's own son, John the Baptist, who will prepare the way for King Jesus.

⌄ Apply

> ❓ *What or who are your enemies?*
> ❓ *What holds you in slavery so that you are unable to serve God in holiness?*
> ❓ *What fears are currently preventing you from wholeheartedly serving God?*
> ❓ *What threatens your relationship with God?*

Think about the revolution in your life that King Jesus has brought. How is he redeeming you from these fears and rescuing you from these enemies?

⌃ Pray

Use Zechariah's song in Luke 1:68-79 to praise God, but personalise the song by adapting the words. Insert your name, and specify the enemies and fears that enslave you. For example, you might give thanks that Jesus enables you "to serve him without fear" of being rejected by other people or without fear for your future security.

Divine government

"When the revolution comes," people say, "then there will be..."

❷ *What one thing would you change if you were in government?*
❷ *What's your motivation for doing that?*

Corrupt governments

In *The Lord of the Rings* by J.R.R. Tolkien, Frodo offers the ring of power to both Gandalf and Galadriel. Gandalf replies: "Don't tempt me. I dare not take it ... I would use this ring from a desire to do good, but through me it would wield power too great and terrible to imagine." And Galadriel says: "Instead of a dark Lord, you would have a queen—beautiful and terrible ... treacherous as the sea ... All shall love me and despair."

Tolkien understands that people are warped and infected by sin. And so the power of human rule is warped and infected by sin. Revolutions start out full of idealism. But time and again in history they have ended up corrupt, unjust and repressive. But how will the revolution of King Jesus be any different?

Jesus' government
Read Isaiah 9:6-7

❷ *What will the revolution of Jesus be like when it is in government?*
❷ *How will it be different from so many other revolutions?*

Jesus will govern in peace with justice and righteousness. And he will govern with justice "for ever". His reign won't start out well and then turn sour. The reason is that Jesus is no ordinary king. He is the "Wonderful Counsellor, Mighty God, Everlasting Father, Prince of Peace".

He is not only the son of David, he is also "the Son of the Most High" (Luke 1:32). He is the God-man who reigns without sin. He reigns in love to rescue and provide for his people. We saw at his first coming how he poured out his love for us, ultimately in his death. And so we can be confident that when he returns to establish his government, he will establish and uphold it with justice and righteousness for ever.

▲ Pray
Read Psalm 72

Psalm 72 is "of Solomon"—the first son of David to reign on David's throne. It points forward to Jesus—the son of David on the throne of David for ever. It describes the kind of king that Jesus is.

Use the words of Psalm 72 to pray, replacing the references to "the king" with Jesus. For example: "May the Lord Jesus be like rain falling on a mown field, like showers watering the earth" (v 6).

Use it as a springboard to pray for your needs, the needs of your church and the needs of the world.

Bible in a year: Nehemiah 4-6 • Luke 19:28-48

Wonderful Counsellor

As Lauren listened to Megan's story her mind switched between sympathy and confusion. Megan spoke about her miscarriage, her bouts of depression, her alienation from church, her anger at God. What could Lauren say to her that would help?

Greg couldn't work out how he and Jess had got into this mess. Three years ago they were happy newlyweds. Now they could hardly exchange a pleasant word. He didn't know what to do...

Jesus: our wisdom

> *He will be called Wonderful Counsellor...*
> (Isaiah 9:6)

Isaiah promises that David's son will be called "Wonderful Counsellor". The kingdom of Israel had got into a mess because it lacked or ignored wise counsel. But God had promised to restore her counsellors (Isaiah 1:26). Now he promises a Wonderful Counsellor-King. The word "wonderful" implies "supernatural". God's King will have God's wisdom. The words of Jesus are divine advice, sound counsel, wisdom to live by.

Read Proverbs 4:18-23

We live in a counselling culture. Lots of people receive counselling. When people have an emotional problem we assume they need a counsellor. Christians already have a Wonderful Counsellor—the Lord Jesus Christ. His words are life and health to us (v 22). Following them is like "the morning sun" (v 18).

Strong Deliverer

Jesus not only gives us sound counsel—he is also our gracious Deliverer! He not only listens to our problems, he sorts them out. Christ Jesus, says Paul, "has become for us wisdom from God—that is, our righteousness, holiness and redemption" (1 Corinthians 1:30). He atones for our guilt, rescues us from our fears, welcomes us into God's family, and promises us a secure future. He promises that one day every tear will be wiped away. Lauren may not be able to diagnose all Megan's problems, but she can talk about Jesus; she can remind Megan of the gospel. And the words of Jesus are "the morning sun".

Greg and Jess have taken steps into deep darkness (Proverbs 4:19). They need to pay attention to Jesus and explore how the desires of their hearts are leading to conflict (v 20, 23 and James 4:1).

⌄ Apply

Above all else, guard your heart, for it is the wellspring of life (Proverbs 4:23).

- ❷ *Give your heart a check-up today. What causes you to get angry, bitter, irritated, frustrated or depressed?*
- ❷ *What do you want in these moments? What do you fear? What are the desires of your heart?*
- ❷ *How do the words of God speak to these desires?*

Worldly wise?

Government ministers all have their "special advisors". Isn't it great to know that every single Christian believer has constant, instant access to the wisest adviser ever?

He will be called Wonderful Counsellor...
(Isaiah 9:6)

King David had a special advisor called Ahithophel. Ahithophel, we are told, gave advice "like that of one who enquires of God" (2 Samuel 16:23). But David's son, King Solomon, goes one better...

A wise king

Read 1 Kings 3:4-28

Solomon didn't need a special advisor. He himself was given "a wise and discerning heart, so that there will never have been anyone like you, nor will there ever be" (v 12). All Israel was in awe of his wisdom (v 28). Indeed, the whole world came to hear it (1 Kings 10:24). Solomon was given wisdom so he could reign righteously. But he was also given wisdom so he could make the ways of God known to the world. The queen of Sheba travelled to honour Solomon because of his famous wisdom. This is wisdom for the world.

Isaiah promises a king like Solomon who won't need special advisors because he himself will be his own "Wonderful Counsellor". Like Solomon, Jesus has wisdom so he can reign righteously, but also so that he can make the ways of God known to the world. The question is: *Will we listen...?*

Wisdom for the world

Jesus said, "The Queen of the South will rise at the judgment with the people of this generation and condemn them, for she came from the ends of the earth to listen to Solomon's wisdom; and now something greater than Solomon is here" (Luke 11:31).

The "Queen of the South" is the queen of Sheba. And the "one greater than Solomon" is Jesus. Jesus is the "Wonderful Counsellor" proclaiming wisdom for the world. But Jesus' hearers reject his words. The queen of Sheba travelled from the ends of the earth to hear Solomon, but they will not listen to one who is greater than Solomon.

⌃ Pray

Pray for the missionaries you know (including yourself!) as they make the wisdom of Jesus known to the world.

What is important for you to know? Maybe you need to keep up to date with developments in your field. Maybe you are studying to gain new skills and qualifications. The most important thing to study is the wisdom of God in the word of God.

❓ *Are you making time for this?*
❓ *What would be the equivalent for you of travelling "from the ends of the earth"?*

The Mighty God

Nick couldn't sleep—he'd lost it again with the kids. They'd been frustratingly disobedient, but his reaction was hardly calm and measured!

What scared him most was how close he had come to lashing out at his boy, Jonah. He felt powerless to control himself.

Nicole was used to being organised, efficient, in control. But her illness had changed everything. Waiting in hospitals. Reliant on others. Her plans rendered meaningless. She felt her life was spiralling out of control.

> *He will be called ... Mighty God*
> (Isaiah 9:6)

From fear to faith

Read Mark 4:35 – 5:43

Isaiah says God's King will be mighty.

- ❓ *How do we see the power of Jesus in each of these stories?*
- ❓ *Over what does he have power?*
- ❓ *How does he drive away our fears?*

Jesus did not heal every sick person or raise every dead body. Neither does he calm all the storms of our lives. The miracles of Jesus are a pointer to God's coming kingdom. God may not sort out all our problems in this life. But in God's coming kingdom we will be "freed from [our] suffering" (5:34).

Mark shows us two ways of living:

1. *The way of fear:* see 4:40-41; 5:15; 5:33 and 5:36.

2. *The way of faith:* see 4:40; 5:34 and 36.

We move away from a life of fear if we believe in Jesus as the Mighty God with power over all things.

Nick needs someone who is mighty—someone who can take control of his life. Nicole needs someone who is mighty—someone she can trust with her future. Think about the specific ways you need a Mighty King like King Jesus. Think of a story about Jesus that shows he is the one who can overcome whatever it is that you are afraid of.

✓ Apply

Jesus tells Jairus, "Don't be afraid; just believe" (5:36). Later on in Mark's Gospel someone says to Jesus: "I do believe; help me overcome my unbelief!" (9:24).

- ❓ *When is it appropriate to say to people—and yourself—"just believe"?*
- ❓ *When might that be a bad idea?*

▲ Pray

Talk to the Lord about your fears, and your struggles to believe he is the Mighty King the specific things that make you afraid.

Pray that you would encourage others today to trust in our Mighty God.

Everlasting

Do you ever get depressed about the state of your own church, and the church in general? Do you wonder whether the message of Jesus will survive?

An everlasting reign

It sometimes seems as if it's only a matter of time before little is left of the church. The forces of atheism, postmodernism and materialism seem too strong.

> *He will be called ... Everlasting Father*
> (Isaiah 9:6)

The coming King, says Isaiah, will be "everlasting". He goes on:

> *Of the increase of his government and peace there will be no end. He will reign on David's throne and over his kingdom ...*
> *from that time on and for ever.* (Isaiah 9:7)

David was Israel's greatest king. But his reign came and went. He died and was buried with his fathers. But the reign of King Jesus will last for ever.

An everlasting King
Read Revelation 1:9-20

❓ *Where is Christ in John's vision (v 13)?*
❓ *What do the lampstands represent (v 20)?*
❓ *What is John's message to struggling churches?*

Jesus reigns for ever because he is an everlasting King. He is "the First and the Last"—he existed before all things and he will exist beyond time. He is "the Living One" who gives life to all things. And he was dead but is "alive for ever and ever!"

He holds "the keys of death" = he has authority over death. Death will never catch up with him for he has already faced death. Death will never overcome him for he has already overcome death.

John was writing to people living under the "eternal" Roman Empire. Some graffiti found in Rome reads: *Rome—your power will never end.* We don't know if it was written in triumph or despair. John writes as a "companion in the suffering and kingdom and patient endurance that are ours in Jesus" (v 9). His message is that Roman power will not last for ever. Jesus—not Rome—is the First and the Last. Jesus will have the last word in history.

> *The seventh angel sounded his trumpet, and there were loud voices in heaven, which said: "The kingdom of the world has become the kingdom of our Lord and of his Messiah, and he will reign for ever and ever."*
> (Revelation 11:15)

···· **TIME OUT** ·······························

Read Acts 2:24-36

❓ *What does Peter say about King David?*
❓ *What does King David say about the promised Christ?*

David spoke of someone who would come back from the grave. But David himself died and was buried. He was speaking of Jesus. God has raised Jesus from death, and made him Lord and King for ever.

Bible in a year: Micah 1-3 • Luke 21:20-38

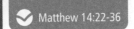
God with us!

"For to us a child is born, to us a son is given …
And he will be called … Mighty God…" (Isaiah 9:6)

This is not the first time Isaiah has spoken of a child and a son. In 7:14 he says, "The virgin will conceive and give birth to a son, and will call him Immanuel". Immanuel means "God with us". The angel who comes to Mary quotes this verse (Matthew 1:23). The baby in the Christmas manger is the Mighty God, Immanuel, God with us.

It's an astonishing claim. So how can we be sure? Some people suggest it's just empty words, or wishful thinking. Others say we're all children of God in some sense and so Jesus was not so special.

God with us
Read Matthew 14:22-36

❓ *What evidence do the Gospels present to us that Jesus is the Mighty God?*

People have healed others through psychosomatic responses, through spirits or through God. But stilling a storm and walking on water are without parallel. Psalm 89:9 says, "You rule over the surging sea; when its waves mount up, you still them". It's talking about God. Only God rules the waves.

Jesus says, "Take courage! It is I!" (Matthew 14:27). The words "It is I" are used in the Greek version of the Old Testament to translate God's revelation of himself as "I AM" (Exodus 3:14). We find the same words in Isaiah 43:10: "I am he. Before me

no god was formed, nor will there be one after me". There will be no new gods before or after the God of Israel so Jesus must be that God. It's clear to the disciples who they have seen: "Those who were in the boat worshipped him, saying, 'Truly you are the Son of God'" (Matthew 14:33).

If Jesus is truly God then it has the following implications:

We have a full revelation of God: If God had not come into the world then we would only ever get someone else's thoughts or ideas about who he is and what he is like. But, in Jesus, God reveals himself through himself. "The Son is the radiance of God's glory and the exact representation of his being" (Hebrews 1:3).

We are fully reconciled with God: Only Jesus the God-man could reconcile both God and humanity, and only as God could his death cover all the sins of his people. "God was reconciling the world to himself in Christ, not counting people's sins against them" (2 Corinthians 5:19).

❓ *How do the disciples respond to Jesus (see Matthew 14:33)?*

🔼 Pray

Pray that you would have time in this busy and joyous day to repeat the disciples' words to those you are celebrating with.

Father

"For to us a child is born, to us a son is given ...
And he will be called ... Everlasting Father..." (Isaiah 9:6)

A son who is called Father—it doesn't seem to make sense!

The Son who reigns like the Father

God was called "Father" in the Old Testament. God is "a father to the fatherless, a defender of widows" who "sets the lonely in families" (Psalm 68:5-6). He has fatherly compassion on those who fear him (Psalm 103:13). And he disciplines his people like a father (Proverbs 3:12). God's people are his son whom he liberates from slavery and oppression (Exodus 4:22-23). The coming King will rule like a father with loving care and discipline. More than that, he will rule like the divine Father. He will care for the fatherless with compassion and liberate his people from the slavery of sin.

The Son who reveals the Father

Read John 14:5-10

Isaiah's promise of a coming child who will be called the Everlasting Father is fulfilled in ways that Isaiah himself could probably not have fully grasped. Jesus says, "I am in the Father, and ... the Father is in me" (v 10). Elsewhere he says, "I and the Father are one" (John 10:30). To know Jesus is to know the Father (14:7). To see Jesus is to see the Father (v 7 and 9). Jesus can be called

the Father because in him, and only in him, the Father is fully known and seen. He is not the Father for there are three distinct Persons in the Godhead. But neither is Jesus separate from the Father for there is one God sharing one being, one will and one love.

"Anyone who has seen me has seen the Father" (v 9). We see what God the Father is like when we look at Jesus.

☑ Apply

❷ *What do we discover about God the Father when we see Jesus?*
❷ *How is this comforting?*

Praise God for his character revealed in Jesus.

···· **TIME OUT** ··

Read John 17:20-23

❷ *How does Jesus describe the unity he has with the Father?*
❷ *What does he pray for the church?*
❷ *Why does he pray this (i.e. what will be the outcome)?*
❷ *How is the prayer of Jesus being answered in your church now?*

⌃ Pray

Make this prayer of the Lord Jesus your own prayer today.

Prince of Peace

"He will be called ... Prince of Peace." (Isaiah 9:6)

David called the son who would inherit his throne Solomon. It means "man of peace". David's reign was a reign of warfare, but by defeating the enemies of God's people he brought peace (2 Samuel 7:1). Solomon's own reign was relatively peaceful, but he sowed the seeds of future conflict. When he was succeeded by his son, Rehoboam, the kingdom fractured into two hostile nations, and over time each was overrun by its enemies. Solomon's reign and kingdom gives a tantalising glimpse of what Isaiah was looking towards, but it did not last for ever.

Now Isaiah promises a new Prince of Peace. In Isaiah 11 he promises that under his reign "the wolf will live with the lamb, the leopard will lie down with the goat, the calf and the lion and the yearling together; and a little child will lead them ... Ephraim's jealousy will vanish, and Judah's enemies will be destroyed; Ephraim will not be jealous of Judah, nor Judah hostile towards Ephraim" (Isaiah 11:6, 13). Ephraim and Judah were names for the different bits of the divided kingdom. God's people will be united and enjoy peace from their enemies. In fact, people from all nations will be united (see Isaiah 19:19-25).

Making peace
Read Colossians 1:19-23

❓ *What has Jesus achieved for us, and how?*

Through Christ, God is going to restore harmony to this fractured universe—to "things on earth or things in heaven" (v 20).

Peace with God

We were once alienated from God. We were his enemies (v 21). But we are reconciled to God through the blood of Jesus (v 22). In a great exchange he took our sin and its penalty on the cross. And he gave us his spotless purity. As a result we can stand before God without accusation (v 22).

Peace with one another
Read Colossians 1:24-27

Paul speaks of a mystery which is now made known to the Gentiles. The mystery is that God is uniting Jews and Gentiles through Christ. The old barriers are broken down for we are equal before the cross: equally guilty and equally forgiven. The mission to the Gentiles is proof that God is uniting all people in Christ.

✓ Apply

We may feel distant from God, and lack the joy of his salvation because of hard-heartedness or unrepented sin. But however we feel, the reality for any genuine believer is that through Christ's blood we are holy and free from accusation (v 23). Will you embrace that truth today?

A great light

Isaiah wrote at a time when the southern kingdom of Judah was threatened by an alliance between the northern kingdom of Israel and Aram (Isaiah 7:1).

God invited the nation and its king, Ahaz, to trust his deliverance (7:3-11). But they chose instead to turn to Assyria for help (7:12). The good news, says Isaiah, is that Assyria will indeed defeat Israel and Aram (7:16 and 8:4). The bad news is that Assyria won't stop there—she will come against Judah (7:17-25 and 8:6-8). And that's only the beginning! God will judge his people by handing them over to their enemies. They will be exiled and defeated. "They will look towards the earth and see only distress and darkness and fearful gloom, and they will be thrust into utter darkness" (8:22). This is the context in which Isaiah promises a son—a coming king.

A light will dawn
Read Isaiah 9:1-7

> ❷ *What does the metaphor of "light" suggest to you?*
> ❷ *Why might this promise be so powerful to Isaiah's first readers?*
> ❷ *How is it different for us now?*

Zebulun, Naphtali and Galilee in the north were the first to fall. The darkness of God's judgment fell on them first. But they will be the first to see the light (v 1-2). With the coming of the dawn, comes the joy of victory and freedom from oppression (v 3-5). The reason for this light, joy, victory and freedom is the promised Son—the King on David's throne who is called "Wonderful

Counsellor, Mighty God, Everlasting Father, Prince of Peace" (v 6-7).

The light has dawned
Read Matthew 4:12-17

> ❷ *How does Matthew see the coming of Jesus to be a fulfilment of this prophesy?*

The exile of Judah was a powerful illustration of God's judgment against all humanity. We are all exiled from God. One day our rebellion will be quashed and judged. We are all living in darkness and heading for utter darkness (Isaiah 8:22). But in the story of Jesus we see the light that the people of Galilee were the first to see. Jesus brings light…

- because he took the darkness we deserve.
- because he defeated the enemies of sin and death.
- because he will reign for ever in joy, peace and justice.

☑ Apply

This is the real message of Christmas! Find some time in the busyness of Christmas holiday celebrations to talk to your friends and family about the real message of the season.

If they are believers, spend some time together praising God that the light has dawned.

Bible in a year: Zechariah 5-8 • Luke 23:1-25

Testing times

This psalm is unique: the only one that gives the circumstances of the writer, but no name. As you read, prepare to flinch before the dreadful description of his plight.

Trouble and why

Read Psalm 102:1-11

Few of us can have faced up to this kind of suffering. Fill in the verses that show his awful situation:

- ill health (v   )
- opposition (v   )
- sorrow (v   )
- loneliness (v   )
- sleeplessness (v   )
- despair (v   )

> ❷ But what, shockingly, does he identify as the source of his trouble (see v 10)?
> ❷ Why is this happening to him?

He recognises that his dreadful plight comes from the hand of God, as a result of his wrath. But notice that his recognition that these ills have come from the wrath of God does not drive him away from the Lord, but rather towards him—to seek his mercy and help.

☑ Apply

We're quick to throw the blame around when things go wrong. "It's my own stupid fault", "I'm under spiritual attack", "We're the victims". But is there another possibility: that God is trying to tell us something?

Confidence in trouble

Read Psalm 102:12-22

> ❷ What brings him hope in trouble (see the contrast between v 11 and 12)?
> ❷ Of what is he supremely confident (see v 13, 15-17, 21)?

He's confident that God is a God who rescues those who are in deepest trouble—and being in that situation himself actually gives him confidence that God will do something about it!

The big picture

Read Psalm 102:23-28

In the moment of deepest despair, the writer's vision clears, and he sees... (Fill in the verses again.)

- God's changelessness (v   )
- that God rules for eternity (v   )
- that he oversees the world he made (v   )
- that he hears the cries of his people, and will draw us into his presence (v   )

☑ Apply

As C.S. Lewis observes, sometimes God uses pain to get through to us when we would otherwise ignore him. Will you accept his "severe mercy" or turn from it in blame and self justification?

Hebrews 1:5, 10-12 suggests who the nameless author of this psalm really is. Read the psalm again, seeing it through his eyes...

A backwards look

As we approach the end of another year it's a great opportunity to reflect on the past and look forward to the future…

Looking back
Read Psalm 103:1-14

❓ *Who is the psalmist singing to?*
❓ *What does he want his listener to do?*
❓ *How is this encouraging for us?*

Notice who this psalm is addressed to: not primarily to God himself, but to David—he cries to *his own soul*, his inmost being (v 1), to praise God. This is good news for us. If you're anything like me, you don't leap out of bed with a song on your lips and joy in your heart. When you settle down to pray, the praise part comes with most difficulty.

David needs to wrestle with his own soul, chiding, arguing and provoking himself to give God his due.

Reasons to rejoice

Take time to list the reasons David gives himself to praise. How has God…

❓ *dealt with him (v 3-5)?*
-
-
-
-

❓ *dealt with the world (v 6-7)?*
-
-

❓ *dealt with our sin (v 10-12)?*
-
-

Now here are powerful reasons to be filled with praise. He does not treat us as we deserve, and his forgiveness is not some half-hearted thing, that leaves us nervous of whether he harbours grudges against us. If you've never memorised verse 12, then now would be a great moment to fix this truth firmly in your mind.

❓ *How does God understand us (v 14)?*
❓ *Why is this so encouraging?*

⌄ Apply

We're tempted to think that because prayer and praise are difficult that we're some-how "not spiritual". The Bible gives ample evidence that such struggling and internal warfare are the signs of truly belonging to God. **Read Romans 7:21-25.**

⌃ Pray

Go through the list above, and praise God for each in turn. If you find it difficult—persevere!

Why not take your diary from this last year and leaf through it to remind yourself of people you've met, and things that have happened—both good and bad: use it to give thanks and praise to God for the way he's dealt with you over the past year.

Thank him that the truth of verse 12 applies to everything you have done wrong this last year, and all the ways you have fallen short.

Bible in a year: Zechariah 13-14 • Luke 24:1-35 ⌄

A forward look

Worry. It afflicts us all in varying degrees from time to time. What will the new year hold? What will happen to my church? Will we survive financially?

Will our children grow towards God this year, or away? Can I survive the pressures of work? Will my health last? David faces the future with great confidence in God—but why? What is his secret?

A realistic view of me
Read Psalm 103:15-22

❷ *How do the truths of verses 15-16 make you feel?*
❷ *What do people in general do with this universal truth?*
❷ *What should Christians do with it?*

We need to cultivate a realistic view of ourselves—we are mortal and we will die. Many people live in denial of this. Everyone jokes about their age, and does their best to hide the signs—hair dye, wrinkle creams, dressing young etc. Believers should be more realistic: knowing that our lives are dust, and that fading and then facing God is inevitable.

A realistic view of God's love

❷ *How do the truths of verses 17-18 make you feel?*
❷ *How does this change our attitude towards verses 15-16?*

Notice the timescale that God's love works to—from everlasting to everlasting! How different from our changing likes and dislikes. Before you were born, God knew you and loved you. And his love stretches beyond the grave to all eternity, guaranteeing our future.

❷ *But what is the condition (v 18)?*

A realistic view of God's sovereignty

❷ *How does the truth of verse 19 change our view of life and death?*
❷ *When do you find this truth most difficult to believe?*

It requires trust to believe this—because the temptation is to believe what we see with our eyes. Chaos and blind chance seem to make some people millionaires and others paupers. But this is the confidence that faith in God brings. Despite the horrors that fill our TV screens, the setbacks we experience and the daily problems we face, true believers know that God is in control—that his throne is unshakeable and that the kingdom of Jesus is being built and will last for ever.

⌃ Pray

Ask God to help you trust him for the coming year, for the future beyond and even for your own death. Commit your year to him.

Look through your diary for the coming year, and talk to God about what you have planned. Praise him for the security that is yours through Christ.

Introduce a friend to

explore

If you're enjoying using *Explore*, why not introduce a friend? *Time with God* is our introduction to daily Bible reading and is a great way to get started with a regular time with God. It includes 28 daily readings along with articles, advice and practical tips on how to apply what the passage teaches.

Why not order a copy for someone you would like to encourage?

Coming up next...

☑ Mark
with Jason Meyer & Katy Morgan

☑ Ezekiel
with Tim Chester

☑ Spiritual healthcheck
with Carl Laferton

☑ Ruth
with Tony Merida & Katy Morgan

 Don't miss your copy. Contact your local Christian bookshop or church agent, or visit:

UK & Europe: thegoodbook.co.uk
info@thegoodbook.co.uk
Tel: 0333 123 0880

North America: thegoodbook.com
info@thegoodbook.com
Tel: 866 244 2165

Australia: thegoodbook.com.au
info@thegoodbook.com.au
Tel: (02) 9564 3555

India: thegoodbook.co.in
contact: @forthetruth.in
Tel: (+91) 8604685533

The Christian Manifesto

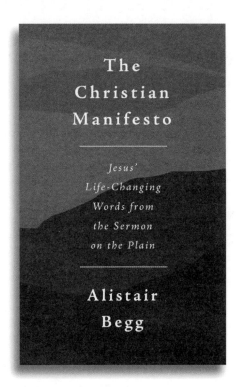

What does genuine Christian living look like in the 21st century, and how can we be motivated to live that way? The answer comes from Jesus' sermon in Luke 6, which starts, "Blessed are you who are poor, for yours is the kingdom of God" and goes on to lay out God's vision statement for the Christian life. It is a manifesto that has nothing to do with politics, culture or personality, but rather God's intentions for his people.

Alistair Begg unpacks this sermon, inviting Christians to live a radically different life that upends the world's values and philosophies. It's a lifestyle that is counterintuitive and countercultural, yet one that God blesses with true meaning and impact.

thegoodbook.co.uk/manifesto
thegoodbook.com/manifesto